GoodFood
magazine

101 VEGGIE DISHES
TRIED-AND-TESTED RECIPES

Editor-in-chief
Orlando Murrin

BBC
BOOKS

Contents

GoodFood magazine

101 VEGGIE DISHES

Published by BBC Worldwide Limited
Woodlands
80 Wood Lane
London W12 0TT

First published 2003
Reprinted in 2003 (twice), 2004 (three times), 2005 (four times), 2006 (twice)
Copyright © BBC Worldwide 2003
All photographs © BBC Good Food Magazine 2003 and
BBC Vegetarian Good Food Magazine 2003

All the recipes contained in this book first appeared in BBC Good
Food Magazine and BBC Vegetarian Good Food Magazine.

ISBN 0 563 48839 5

Edited by Gilly Cubitt

Commissioning Editor: Vivien Bowler
Project Editor: Sarah Miles
Designers: Kathryn Gammon and Annette Peppis
Design Manager: Sarah Ponder
Production Controller: Christopher Tinker

Set in Helvetica and ITC Officina Sans
Printed and bound in Italy by LEGO SpA
Colour origination by Radstock Reproductions Ltd, Midsomer Norton

Introduction

Conjuring up vegetarian dishes, whether you're a lifelong devotee or someone who wants a change for one night, is not as simple as just leaving out the meat. As vegetarians know, there's much more to veggie cooking than a cheese omelette or a mushroom risotto.

That's why we've picked our all-time favourite recipes from *BBC Good Food Magazine* for this compact but comprehensive book. It's got all those simple-but-delectable vegetarian recipes you always wish you had up your sleeve. We think you'll find it invaluable whatever the occasion, with ideas on light snacks, mains and puds, plus the trickiest dishes of all – dairy-free.

All the recipes have been tested in the Good Food kitchen, guaranteeing you success every time. They're also well balanced and come with a nutritional breakdown so you can keep track of the calorie, fat and salt content.

As always, our recipes make the most of vegetables in season plus good use of storecupboard and frozen vegetables, which count towards your five-a-day recommended portions of fruit and vegetables. So, not only will you wow family and friends with fabulous food, like the *Spicy Nasi Goreng* pictured opposite (see page 116 for recipe), they'll be getting healthy, balanced meals into the bargain.

Orlando Murrin

Editor, *BBC Good Food Magazine*

Conversion tables

NOTES ON THE RECIPES
• Eggs are medium in the UK and Australia (large in America) unless stated otherwise.
• Wash all fresh produce before preparation.

OVEN TEMPERATURES

Gas	°C	Fan °C	°F	Oven temp.
¼	110	90	225	Very cool
½	120	100	250	Very cool
1	140	120	275	Cool or slow
2	150	130	300	Cool or slow
3	160	140	325	Warm
4	180	160	350	Moderate
5	190	170	375	Moderately hot
6	200	180	400	Fairly hot
7	220	200	425	Hot
8	230	210	450	Very hot
9	240	220	475	Very hot

APPROXIMATE WEIGHT CONVERSIONS
• All the recipes in this book list both imperial and metric measurements. Conversions are approximate and have been rounded up or down. Follow one set of measurements only; do not mix the two.
• Cup measurements, which are used by cooks in Australia and America, have not been listed here as they vary from ingredient to ingredient. Please use kitchen scales to measure dry/solid ingredients.

SPOON MEASURES

- Spoon measurements are level unless otherwise specified.
- 1 teaspoon = 5ml
- 1 tablespoon = 15ml
- 1 Australian tablespoon = 20ml (cooks in Australia should measure 3 teaspoons where 1 tablespoon is specified in a recipe)

APPROXIMATE LIQUID CONVERSIONS

metric	imperial	AUS	US
50ml	2fl oz	¼ cup	¼ cup
125ml	4fl oz	½ cup	½ cup
175ml	6fl oz	¾ cup	¾ cup
225ml	8fl oz	1 cup	1 cup
300ml	10fl oz/½ pint	½ pint	1¼ cups
450ml	16fl oz	2 cups	2 cups/1 pint
600ml	20fl oz/1 pint	1 pint	2½ cups
1 litre	35fl oz/1¾ pints	1¾ pints	1 quart

A velvety smooth soup with a dramatic
colour but gentle flavour.

Spinach, Sage and Potato Soup

50g/2oz butter
2 red onions, chopped
3 garlic cloves, crushed
15g fresh sage, shredded,
plus extra to garnish
2 large potatoes (about 500g/
1lb 2oz), diced
1.4 litres/2½ pints vegetable stock
250g/9oz baby spinach leaves
4 tbsp crème fraîche,
to serve (optional)

Takes 40 minutes • Serves 4

1 Melt the butter in a large pan and fry the onions for 5–6 minutes over a low heat until softened slightly. Add the garlic, sage and potatoes, cover and cook over a very low heat for 10 minutes.
2 Stir in the stock, bring to the boil and cook for 5 minutes. Add the spinach and cook for 2 minutes. Transfer the mixture to a food processor or blender and whizz until smooth (you may need to do this in batches).
3 Return to the pan and heat gently until warmed. Season to taste and serve with a spoonful of crème fraîche, if using, garnished with the extra sage.

• Per serving 265 kcalories, protein 7g, carbohydrate 28g, fat 14g, saturated fat 9g, fibre 4g, added sugar none, salt 1.67g

Choose the least knobbly celeriac
you can find to keep waste to a minimum.

Celeriac and Blue Cheese Soup

25g/1oz butter
1 medium onion, chopped
750g/1lb 10oz celeriac, peeled and
cut into 2cm/¾in chunks
1 large baking potato, chopped
2 tbsp chopped fresh sage leaves
600ml/1 pint vegetable stock
300ml/½ pint single cream
225g/8oz vegetarian blue cheese
(eg stilton or dolcelatte), diced
fresh chives and deep-fried sage
leaves, to garnish (optional)

Takes 35 minutes • Serves 4

1 Melt the butter in a large pan and gently fry the vegetables and sage for 5 minutes. Stir in the stock and bring to the boil. Cover and simmer for 15 minutes until the vegetables are tender.
2 Transfer to a food processor and whizz until smooth (you may need to do this in batches). Return the soup to the pan and stir in the single cream and half the blue cheese. Cook over a low heat until the cheese has melted, but do not allow to boil. Season to taste.
3 Divide the soup between serving bowls and sprinkle with the remaining blue cheese, the chives and deep-fried sage leaves, if liked, to serve.

• Per serving 488 kcalories, protein 17g, carbohydrate 27g, fat 35g, saturated fat 22g, fibre 9g, added sugar none, salt 2.78g

The rice will continue to absorb the stock after the soup is cooked.
If you reheat the soup you may need to add more stock.

Spring Greens and Rice Soup

1 tbsp olive oil
1 onion, chopped
2 garlic cloves, crushed
100g/4oz risotto rice
finely grated zest and juice
of 1 lemon
1.4 litres/2½ pints vegetable stock
2 large firm tomatoes, seeded
and chopped
225g/8oz spring greens, stalks
removed and shredded
120g jar vegetarian pesto sauce
vegetarian parmesan shavings,
to garnish

Takes 35 minutes • Serves 4

1 Heat the oil in a large pan and fry the onion and garlic for 3–4 minutes until softened. Stir in the rice and cook for 1 minute, stirring occasionally.
2 Add the lemon zest and juice and stock. Bring to the boil and simmer for 15 minutes.
3 Stir the tomatoes, greens and pesto into the soup. Bring to the boil and simmer for 4–5 minutes until the rice is tender. Season to taste and serve sprinkled with the parmesan shavings.

• Per serving 409 kcalories, protein 12g, carbohydrate 33g, fat 26g, saturated fat 5g, fibre 3g, added sugar none, salt 1.93g

If you can't buy fresh lemongrass, most supermarkets stock it minced in jars. Substitute a teaspoon of this instead.

Hot Sour Corn Soup

1 corn on the cob
1 tbsp vegetable oil
1 red chilli, seeded and sliced
1 shallot, finely chopped
2 stalks lemongrass, bruised
3 baby leeks or spring onions, sliced
1 red pepper, seeded and thinly sliced
400ml can coconut milk
850ml/1½ pints vegetable stock
2 kaffir lime leaves (optional)
175g/6oz thread egg noodles
juice of 1 lime
small bunch coriander, roughly chopped

Takes 35 minutes • Serves 4

1 Hold the corn cob upright on a board, and, using a sharp knife, slice downwards to strip the corn kernels from the cob. Heat the oil in a large pan, add the kernels, chilli, shallot, lemongrass, leeks or spring onions and red pepper, and cook for 3–4 minutes, stirring occasionally.

2 Add the coconut milk, stock and lime leaves, if using. Bring to the boil, then cover. Reduce the heat and simmer gently for 15 minutes. Discard the lemongrass stalks. Add the noodles and cook for 4 minutes until tender.

3 Remove from the heat and stir in the lime juice and coriander. Season with salt, if necessary, and serve immediately.

• Per serving 545 kcalories, protein 11g, carbohydrate 41g, fat 39g, saturated fat 27g, fibre 9g, added sugar none, salt 0.97g

Saffron lends a splash of sunshine colour and flavour to
a simple leek soup, topped with crispy leek rings.

Saffron and Leek Soup

4 medium leeks
50g/2oz butter
1 tbsp olive oil
good pinch of saffron strands
2 tbsp plain flour
1.2 litres/2 pints vegetable stock
oil, for shallow frying
1 tbsp cornflour
1 medium egg white, lightly beaten
2 spring onions, diagonally sliced

Takes 35 minutes • Serves 4

1 Cut a 7.5cm/3in length of leek into slices. Separate into rings and set aside. Chop the remaining leeks. Heat the butter and oil in a large pan and cook the leeks for 1 minute, stirring. Mix in the saffron and flour, then gradually stir in the stock, bring to the boil and simmer gently for 10 minutes, until thickened, stirring frequently.
2 Transfer the soup to a food processor and whizz until smooth. You may need to do this in batches. Return to the clean pan and season to taste. Heat through gently.
3 Meanwhile, heat a little oil in a frying pan. Toss the leek rings in the cornflour. Shake off the excess, then dip the rings into the egg white. Fry the leek rings until crisp and golden. Drain and serve scattered over the soup along with the spring onion.

• Per serving 219 kcalories, protein 4g, carbohydrate 12g, fat 17g, saturated fat 7g, fibre 2g, added sugar none, salt 1.34g

The flavours of tomatoes and white wine work
really well with celery in this warm salad.

Celery and White Bean Salad

50g/2oz butter
1½ heads of celery, sliced diagonally
1 tbsp chopped fresh rosemary
150ml/¼ pint dry white wine
150ml/¼ pint vegetable stock
pinch of saffron strands
450g/1lb tomatoes, skinned, seeded
and cut into wedges
finely grated zest and juice
of ½ lemon
410g can cannellini beans,
drained and rinsed
50g/2oz pitted black olives
handful of flatleaf parsley,
roughly torn
crusty bread, to serve

Takes 40 minutes • Serves 4

1 Melt the butter in a large pan and add the celery and rosemary. Cover and cook gently for 10 minutes, until soft but not browned.
2 Stir in the wine, stock and saffron. Bring to the boil and boil for 8–10 minutes, until the liquid has reduced by half.
3 Stir in the tomatoes, lemon zest and juice and cannellini beans. Bring to the boil and simmer for 5 minutes. Stir in the olives and season to taste. Allow to cool slightly. Scatter with parsley and serve with crusty bread to mop up the juices.

• Per serving 262 kcalories, protein 9g, carbohydrate 23g, fat 13g, saturated fat 7g, fibre 9g, added sugar none, salt 2.32g

Tangy kumquats contrast with the earthy
flavours of the mushrooms and sweet red onion.

Hot Mushroom and Kumquat Salad

5 tbsp olive oil
250g/9oz mixed mushrooms,
(eg field, shiitake, chestnut),
sliced
1 red onion, sliced
50g/2oz kumquats, sliced
pinch of dried chilli flakes
50g/2oz sliced white bread, crusts
removed and cubed
85g/3oz rocket
1 tbsp white wine vinegar

Takes 30 minutes • Serves 2
(easily doubled)

1 Melt one tablespoon of the oil in a frying pan and fry the mushrooms for 2–3 minutes. Add the onion and kumquats and fry for a further 2–3 minutes. Set aside and keep warm.

2 Mix together the chilli flakes, bread cubes and one tablespoon of the oil. Season well. Heat one tablespoon of oil in the frying pan and fry the bread mixture until crisp and golden. Divide the rocket between serving plates and top with the mushroom and kumquat mix and the chilli croûtons.

3 Whisk together the last of the oil with the vinegar, season, and drizzle over the salad. Serve immediately.

• Per serving 488 kcalories, protein 6g, carbohydrate 19g, fat 39g, saturated fat 6g, fibre 4g, added sugar none, salt 0.46g

Use less salty Lancashire cheese in
place of feta, if you prefer.

Two Cheese Salad with Croûtons

2 thick slices white bread,
crusts removed
1 tsp paprika
2 tbsp olive oil
1 garlic clove, crushed
1 large cos or romaine lettuce
2 ripe avocados
2 tbsp lemon juice
1 large courgette, cut into sticks
140g/5oz feta, crumbled into chunks
25g/1oz finely grated parmesan
6 tbsp olive oil dressing
(ready-made)

Takes 30 minutes • Serves 4

1 Preheat the oven to 220°C/Gas 7/fan oven 200°C. Cut the bread into 2cm/¾in cubes. Toss with the paprika, olive oil and garlic, then spread out on a baking sheet. Bake for 7–8 minutes, until crisp.

2 Tear the lettuce into large pieces. Peel and slice the avocados and toss with lemon juice and freshly ground black pepper.

3 Mix the lettuce, courgette, feta or Lancashire cheese and croûtons. Put into a large salad bowl with the avocado, and sprinkle with parmesan. Drizzle olive oil dressing over the salad to serve.

• Per serving 453 kcalories, protein 12g, carbohydrate 12g, fat 40g, saturated fat 10g, fibre 4g, added sugar none, salt 1.92g

A fresh-tasting salad made from summer
vegetables, crumbly cheese and mint.

English Garden Salad

500g/1lb 2oz new potatoes,
sliced thickly
350g/12oz runner beans, sliced
a bunch of spring onions, chopped
240g tub sunblush or sun-dried
tomatoes, drained
225g/8oz Cheshire or
Lancashire cheese
a good handful of fresh mint leaves,
roughly chopped
4–5 tbsp bought honey and
mustard dressing

Takes 30 minutes • Serves 4

1 Cook the potatoes in salted boiling water
for 7 minutes. Add the beans to the pan
and cook for a further 7–9 minutes, until the
potatoes and beans are just tender.
2 Drain the vegetables and rinse under cold
running water to stop them cooking. Shake
the colander to get rid of as much water as
possible, then tip into a large bowl. Add the
onions and tomatoes, crumble in the cheese
and mix well.
3 Add most of the mint and dressing
and toss everything lightly together. Tip into
a serving dish, drizzle with a little more
dressing and scatter over the rest of the
mint.

• Per serving 427 kcalories, protein 18g, carbohydrate
29g, fat 27g, saturated fat 11g, fibre 6g, added sugar
none, salt 2.39g

Check the cheese counter in the supermarket for jars of marinated feta in oil. Use the oil for the dressing.

Feta and Griddled Peach Salad

juice of 1 lime
4 fresh ripe peaches, each cut into wedges
200g bag mixed salad leaves
300g jar marinated feta in oil
1 red onion, sliced
2 tbsp chopped fresh mint

Takes 10 minutes • Serves 4

1 Heat a lightly greased griddle pan until very hot. Squeeze the lime juice over the peaches and place them on the griddle pan. Cook them for 2–3 minutes, turning, until nicely charred.
2 In a large salad bowl, mix together the salad leaves, feta, two tablespoons of the oil from the feta, the red onion and chopped mint. Season well.
3 Divide between plates and top with the charred peaches. Sprinkle over black pepper and serve.

• Per serving 272 kcalories, protein 11g, carbohydrate 11g, fat 21g, saturated fat 9g, fibre 2g, added sugar none, salt 2.32g

Choose a small soft goat's cheese. The rind is edible but discard the ends to make four matching slices.

Goat's Cheese Salad

100g/4oz soft goat's cheese
1 oval bread roll, cut into 4 slices and ends discarded
4 tsp olive oil
1 tsp lemon juice or white wine vinegar
½ tsp wholegrain or Dijon mustard
1 garlic clove, chopped
handful of mixed salad leaves

Takes 10 minutes • Serves 1
(easily multiplied)

1 Preheat the grill to high. Cut the cheese into four slices. Toast the bread slices on both sides, then top with the cheese.
2 Sprinkle with black pepper and a little of the olive oil and grill for 2–3 minutes.
3 Meanwhile, mix together the remaining olive oil, lemon juice or vinegar, mustard and garlic. Season, then toss with the salad leaves. Pile on to a plate and top with the cheese toasts.

• Per serving 509 kcalories, protein 19g, carbohydrate 16g, fat 42g, saturated fat 15g, fibre 1g, added sugar none, salt 1.84g

Use authentic Greek feta for the best flavour. It keeps for about six months unopened in the fridge, so it's a great supper standby.

Feta and Flageolet Salad

100g/4oz baby spinach leaves
300g/10oz large salad tomatoes, cut into wedges
400g can flageolet or cannellini beans, drained and rinsed
1 small red onion, finely chopped
200g pack feta
crusty bread, to serve

FOR THE DRESSING
1 garlic clove, finely chopped
1 tbsp lemon juice
1 tsp clear honey
3 tbsp olive oil

Takes 10–20 minutes • Serves 4

1 Cover a large platter or shallow dish with the spinach leaves. Scatter the tomato wedges over the spinach, followed by the beans and red onion.
2 Drain off the liquid from the pack of feta and crumble the cheese over the vegetables.
3 Tip the dressing ingredients into a small bowl, season and whisk with a fork until slightly thickened. Drizzle over the salad, and serve with crusty bread.

• Per serving 515 kcalories, protein 31g, carbohydrate 56g, fat 20g, saturated fat 8g, fibre 19g, added sugar 1g, salt 2.05g

The traditional combination of tomatoes, olives and feta cheese is made more substantial by the addition of pasta.

Greek Pasta Salad

300g/10oz fusilli (spirals) or farfalle (butterflies) or penne (quill tubes)
225g bag prepared fresh baby spinach leaves
250g punnet cherry tomatoes, halved
100g/4oz kalamata olives
225g/8oz feta, broken into rough chunks
3 tbsp olive oil
crusty bread, to serve

Takes 30 minutes • Serves 4

1 Tip the pasta into a large pan of salted boiling water and boil for 10 minutes. Throw in the spinach, stir well and boil for another 2 minutes. Drain into a colander or sieve and leave to drip dry.
2 Tip the tomatoes, olives and feta into a large bowl, grind lots of black pepper over and then drizzle with the olive oil.
3 Toss in the drained pasta and spinach, and serve with crusty bread.

• Per serving 418 kcalories, protein 18g, carbohydrate 37g, fat 23g, saturated fat 8g, fibre 5g, added sugar 0.1g, salt 3.48g

Tzatziki is Greek yogurt and cucumber salad,
usually eaten as a dip for pitta bread.

Beetroot and Tzatziki Sandwich

knob of softened butter
2 thick slices mixed-seed bread
3 tbsp Greek yogurt
4cm/1½in piece cucumber, grated
and drained
2 tbsp chopped fresh mint, plus
extra leaves to garnish
handful of mixed salad leaves
1 small cooked beetroot, sliced

Takes 10 minutes • Serves 1
(easily multiplied)

1 Spread the softened butter over one side of each slice of bread.
2 To make the tzatziki, mix together the Greek yogurt, grated cucumber and chopped mint in a small bowl. Season well.
3 Place a handful of mixed salad leaves on each slice of bread. Arrange the beetroot slices on top of the salad leaves and spoon over the cucumber tzatziki. Sprinkle with the extra fresh mint leaves.

• Per serving 433 kcalories, protein 13g, carbohydrate 60g, fat 18g, saturated fat 11g, fibre 2g, added sugar none, salt 1.63g

Muffins make instant pizza bases. Use pesto in place of pizza topping sauce if you have some handy.

Mini Muffin Pizzas

1 very small courgette
1 toasting muffin
2 tbsp ready-made pizza topping or passata (sieved tomatoes)
2 sun-dried tomatoes, thinly sliced
40g/1½oz feta, cubed
1 tsp torn fresh oregano leaves
2 tsp olive oil

Takes 15 minutes • Serves 1
(easily multiplied)

1 Preheat the grill to medium. Using a potato peeler, peel the courgette lengthways into thin ribbons.
2 Split the muffin in half. Spread the cut halves with the pizza topping or passata and toast for 1–2 minutes until hot.
3 Arrange the courgettes over the muffin halves. Top with the sun-dried tomatoes, feta and oregano. Season. Drizzle with the olive oil and grill for 2 minutes.

• Per serving 448 kcalories, protein 15g, carbohydrate 39g, fat 27g, saturated fat 9g, fibre 3g, added sugar 1g, salt 1.81g

Grill the halloumi cheese until just golden and eat it
immediately as it becomes chewy when it cools.

Halloumi and Tomato Pitta

2 cos lettuce leaves, shredded
1 plum tomato, sliced
1 thin slice sweet onion, separated
into rings
1 sprig fresh mint, chopped
1 tsp olive oil
3 thick slices halloumi
1 pitta bread

Takes 10 minutes • Serves 1
(easily multiplied)

1 Preheat the grill to high. Put the lettuce, tomato slices, onion rings and mint in a bowl, toss together with the olive oil and season.

2 Place the halloumi slices on a baking sheet and grill for about 2 minutes until turning golden, then turn over and grill for a further minute.

3 Grill the pitta pocket for a few seconds on each side until it puffs open. Tuck the cheese and salad inside the pitta and eat immediately.

• Per serving 375 kcalories, protein 16g, carbohydrate 46g, fat 15g, saturated fat 7g, fibre 3g, added sugar none, salt 1.45g

Turn ordinary sliced white bread into garlicky
crispbreads for these warm sandwiches.

Ricotta-stuffed Crispbreads

8 slices white bread, crusts removed
50g/2oz garlic butter, melted
3 tbsp olive oil
1 red and 1 yellow pepper, halved,
seeded and chopped
225g/8oz cavolo nero or savoy
cabbage, torn
225g/8oz cherry tomatoes, halved
1 tbsp white wine vinegar
250g tub ricotta cheese
handful of basil, plus fresh basil,
to serve

Takes 20 minutes • Serves 4

1 Preheat the oven to 200°C/Gas 6/fan oven
180°C. Roll out each slice of bread until
flattened. Place on baking sheets and brush
with the garlic butter. Bake for 10 minutes
until crisp.
2 Heat two tablespoons of the oil in a
pan, add the peppers and cook until lightly
charred. Add the cavolo nero or savoy
cabbage and cook for 2–3 minutes. Remove
from the heat and add the tomatoes, vinegar
and seasoning. Mix the ricotta cheese and
basil.
3 Spread four of the bread slices with the
ricotta mixture. Top with the vegetables and
place another slice of bread on top. Drizzle
with the remaining olive oil and garnish with
the fresh basil.

• Per serving 385 kcalories, protein 10g, carbohydrate
21g, fat 30g, saturated fat 13g, fibre 4g, added sugar
0.2g, salt 0.7g

If you can't find purple sprouting broccoli,
use green broccoli cut into thin florets.

Broccoli and Poached Egg Toasts

225g/8oz purple sprouting broccoli
1 ciabatta loaf
1 garlic clove, halved
2 tbsp olive oil
1 tbsp Dijon mustard
6 shallots, halved lengthways
4 large eggs

Takes 25 minutes • Serves 4

1 Slice the broccoli and blanch in boiling water for 1 minute. Drain and refresh in cold water. Dry on kitchen paper. Heat a griddle or frying pan.
2 Cut the ciabatta in half horizontally, then cut each slice in half. Rub with the garlic and brush with half the oil. Cook the ciabatta on the griddle for 1–2 minutes on each side until golden. Spread with the mustard and keep warm. Toss the shallots in the remaining olive oil and cook cut-side down on the griddle for 2 minutes on each side. Keep warm.
3 Pile the broccoli on to the griddle and cook for 3–4 minutes, turning frequently. Meanwhile, poach the eggs in gently simmering water until set to your liking. Pile the shallots and broccoli on the ciabatta. Top with the eggs and season.

• Per serving 380 kcalories, protein 17g, carbohydrate 47g, fat 15g, saturated fat 3g, fibre 4g, added sugar none, salt 1.49g

You should find all these ingredients at the delicatessen counter. Buy some good bread to go with it.

Olive and Ricotta Pâté

450g/1lb ricotta cheese
50g/2oz vegetarian parmesan, finely grated
2 medium egg whites, lightly beaten
190g jar lemon and mint marinated green olives
185g can pitted black olives, drained
4 sun-dried tomatoes, roughly chopped
2 sprigs fresh rosemary, leaves only
bread and roasted tomatoes, to serve

Takes 40 minutes • Serves 6

1 Preheat the oven to 200°C/Gas 6/fan oven 180°C. Oil and base line a 20cm/8in sandwich tin. In a large bowl, beat together the ricotta, parmesan, egg whites and seasoning.
2 Spoon into the prepared cake tin and level the surface with the back of a wet spoon. Press the olives, sun-dried tomatoes and rosemary into the surface and bake for 25–30 minutes until firm.
3 Turn out and remove the paper. Serve in wedges with bread and roasted tomatoes.

• Per serving 227 kcalories, protein 12g, carbohydrate 3g, fat 19g, saturated fat 8g, fibre 2g, added sugar none, salt 4.07g

This is a wonderfully creamy mixture yet the
fresh flavours of the vegetables still shine through.

Minted Spring Vegetables

25g/1oz butter
1 tbsp olive oil
225g/8oz baby onions
200ml/7fl oz dry white wine
2 medium leeks, halved and cut into
5cm/2in ribbons
350g/12oz frozen petits pois
3 heads of baby gem lettuce,
quartered lengthways
200ml/7fl oz crème fraîche
2 tbsp chopped fresh mint
2 tbsp chopped fresh flatleaf parsley
bulghar wheat or couscous, to serve

Takes 35 minutes • Serves 4

1 Heat the butter and olive oil in a large non-stick frying pan until lightly foaming. Add the baby onions and cook over a low heat for 8 minutes. Add the wine and leeks and bring to the boil. Simmer for 5 minutes until the leeks are tender.
2 Add the petits pois and simmer for a further 5 minutes. Add the lettuce and simmer for a further 3 minutes.
3 Stir in the crème fraîche and herbs. Season well and warm through very gently for 2–3 minutes. Serve spooned over hot, soaked bulghar wheat or steamed couscous.

• Per serving 321 kcalories, protein 9g, carbohydrate 18g, fat 20g, saturated fat 10g, fibre 8g, added sugar none, salt 0.23g

Sounds strange, but take the pan off the heat before you add the salad ingredients and you'll love the fresh-tasting result.

Stir-fried Salad with Almonds

3 tbsp olive oil
85g/3oz whole blanched almonds
1 bunch spring onions, sliced
1 small cucumber, seeded and sliced
3 sticks celery, cut into batons
225g/8oz small tomatoes, quartered
2 little gem lettuces, torn in pieces
25g/1oz watercress
25g/1oz fresh coriander
juice of ½ lemon
½ tsp sugar
crusty bread or boiled rice, to serve

Takes 15 minutes • Serves 4

1 Heat two tablespoons of the oil in a frying pan or wok and fry the almonds for 2–3 minutes until golden. Drain on kitchen paper then chop roughly.
2 Add the remaining oil to the pan and when hot, add the spring onions, cucumber, celery and tomatoes and stir fry for 2 minutes. Remove from the heat, add the remaining ingredients and toss together until combined. Season.
3 Spoon the warm salad on to serving plates and scatter the almonds over. Spoon the pan juices over and serve with crusty bread or boiled rice, if liked.

• Per serving 247 kcalories, protein 6g, carbohydrate 6g, fat 22g, saturated fat 2g, fibre 3g, added sugar 1g, salt 0.09g

Blinis make brilliant bases for canapés and starters.
Try them with herby cream cheese, tomatoes and rocket too.

Vegetable Blini Stacks

225g/8oz asparagus
spears, trimmed
100g/4oz sugarsnap peas
140g/5oz broccoli florets
250g crème fraîche
1½ tbsp fresh vegetarian pesto
handful of fresh basil, roughly torn
8 large, ready-made blinis
(about 10cm/4in diameter)
140g/5oz semi-dried
tomatoes, drained

Takes 20 minutes • Serves 4

1 Preheat the oven to 180°C/Gas 4/fan oven 160°C. Bring a large pan of salted water to the boil. Add the asparagus, sugarsnap peas and broccoli and cook for 2 minutes until just tender. Drain and set aside. Combine the crème fraîche, pesto and half the basil. Season to taste.
2 Place four blinis on a large ovenproof dish. Top with the vegetables and tomatoes and spoon over the crème fraîche mixture.
3 Halve the remaining blinis and place on top of the vegetables. Bake for 8 minutes until heated through.

• Per serving 372 kcalories, protein 10g, carbohydrate 20g, fat 28g, saturated fat 13g, fibre 4g, added sugar none, salt 0.43g

Sounds exotic but frozen stir fry vegetables plus coconut and Thai curry paste add up to a tasty Thai-style meal.

Thai Coconut Vegetable Soup

1 tbsp vegetable oil
25g/1oz fresh root ginger, peeled and sliced
2 garlic cloves, sliced
2 lemongrass stalks, bruised
3–4 bird's eye chillies, bruised
4 kaffir lime leaves, bruised
400ml can coconut milk
200ml carton coconut cream
500g/1lb 2oz mixed stir fry vegetables
fresh basil and coriander leaves, to garnish

Takes 30 minutes • Serves 3

1 Heat the oil in a frying pan or wok and stir fry the ginger, garlic, lemongrass and chillies for 30 seconds.
2 Add the lime leaves to the pan and pour the coconut milk and cream over. Bring to the boil, cover and simmer gently for about 15 minutes, stirring occasionally.
3 Add the vegetables to the pan and return to the boil. Simmer for 2–3 minutes, stirring frequently, until the vegetables are just tender. Ladle into bowls and serve topped with the fresh basil and coriander.

• Per serving 917 kcalories, protein 11g, carbohydrate 20g, fat 80g, saturated fat 72g, fibre 18g, added sugar 1g, salt 0.18g

Curry can be deceivingly high in fat – this version is packed
with flavour and has only 5g fat per serving.

Spicy Vegetable Chapati Wraps

300g/10oz sweet potatoes, peeled
and roughly cubed
400g can peeled plum tomatoes
400g can chickpeas, drained
½ tsp dried chilli flakes
2 tbsp mild curry paste
100g/4oz baby spinach leaves
2 tbsp chopped fresh coriander
4 plain chapatis (Indian flatbreads)
4 tbsp fat-free Greek yogurt

Takes 25 minutes • Serves 4

1 Cook the sweet potatoes in salted boiling water for 10–12 minutes until tender. Meanwhile, put the tomatoes, chickpeas, chilli flakes and curry paste in another pan and simmer gently for about 5 minutes, stirring all the time.

2 Preheat the grill. Drain the sweet potatoes and add to the tomato mixture. Stir in the spinach and cook for a minute until just starting to wilt. Stir in the coriander, season to taste and keep warm.

3 Sprinkle the chapatis with a little water and grill for 20–30 seconds each side. Spoon on the filling, top with yoghurt and fold in half to serve.

• Per serving 289 kcalories, protein 12g, carbohydrate 54g, fat 5g, saturated fat none, fibre 5g, added sugar none, salt 1.08g

A simple potato cake makes a welcome change
from toast with your fried egg.

Rösti with Egg and Onions

4 tsp olive oil
½ red or white onion, finely sliced
50g/2oz potato, coarsely grated
1 tsp wholegrain mustard
1 medium egg
2 tomatoes, sliced
drizzle of balsamic vinegar

Takes 15 minutes • Serves 1
(easily multiplied)

1 Heat half the oil in a non-stick frying pan. Fry half the onion until crispy. Drain and reserve. Mix the potato with the rest of the onion, mustard and seasoning.
2 Add the remaining oil to the pan, add the potato mixture and press into a 12cm/4½in round. Fry for 8–10 minutes until golden, turning several times. Fry the egg alongside the rösti.
3 Arrange the tomatoes on a plate and drizzle with the balsamic vinegar. Serve the rösti on the tomatoes with the egg and crispy onion on top.

• Per serving 335 kcalories, protein 9g, carbohydrate 16g, fat 27g, saturated fat 4g, fibre 3g, added sugar none, salt 0.53g

Tapenade is a thick purée of olives, capers,
garlic and olive oil (but watch out for hidden anchovies).

Souffléd Avocado Omelette

3 medium eggs, separated
1 tbsp milk
2 tbsp chopped fresh flatleaf parsley
2 tsp olive oil
2 tbsp vegetarian black
olive tapenade
1 small avocado, halved,
stoned and sliced
juice of ½ lemon
tomato salad, to serve (optional)

Takes 10 minutes • Serves 4

1 Place the egg whites in a large bowl and
whisk to soft peaks. Place the egg yolks in
a separate bowl with the milk and parsley.
Season and beat together. Add a quarter
of the whites to the yolks and gently stir.
Fold in the remaining egg whites.
2 Preheat the grill to high. Heat the oil in a
20cm/8in non-stick frying pan. Add the egg
mixture and cook for 2–3 minutes until lightly
set. Place under the grill for 1–2 minutes to
cook the top.
3 Spoon the olive tapenade over one half
of the omelette. Top with the avocado and
squeeze over the lemon juice. Fold over the
other half, transfer to a plate and serve with
a tomato salad, if liked.

• Per serving 717 kcalories, protein 21g, carbohydrate
21g, fat 70g, saturated fat 12g, fibre 4g, added sugar
none, salt 2.39g

As the name suggests there's no pastry,
just chunky vegetables set in egg.

Crustless Vegetable Quiche

1 tbsp vegetable oil
1 yellow and 1 orange pepper, cut
into quarters and seeded
2 courgettes, cut into chunks
2 large red onions, cut into wedges
4 medium eggs, beaten
100ml/3½fl oz milk
2 tbsp fresh vegetarian pesto sauce
green salad, to serve

Takes 40 minutes • Serves 4

1 Preheat the oven to 200°C/Gas 6/fan
oven 180°C. Heat the oil in a wok or large
frying pan and stir fry the peppers, courgettes
and onions over a high heat for 2–3 minutes.
2 Transfer the vegetables to an oiled 2 litre/
3½ pint ovenproof dish. In a large bowl,
mix together the eggs, milk, pesto and
seasoning.
3 Pour over the vegetables and bake for
25 minutes until firm to the touch in the
centre. Serve warm with a crisp green leaf
salad.

• Per serving 211 kcalories, protein 9g, carbohydrate
10g, fat 15g, saturated fat 3g, fibre 2g, added sugar
none, salt 0.36g

A 'cut and come again' tart, which will keep
in the fridge for up to three days.

Tomato and Chive Tart

340g pack shortcrust pastry
200ml tub full or half fat
crème fraîche
2 eggs
2 tbsp green or red pesto
6 ripe tomatoes, sliced
225g/8oz cherry tomatoes, halved
snipped fresh chives
green salad, to serve

Takes 35 minutes • Serves 6

1 Preheat the oven to 220°C/Gas 7/fan
200°C. Roll out the pastry and use to line
the base and sides of a Swiss roll tin (about
23 × 33cm/9 × 13in).
2 Mix the crème fraîche, eggs and pesto
then season. Pour this creamy mixture over
the pastry. Scatter both kinds of tomato on
top, then season and bake for 20 minutes
until set.
3 Toss on some chives and serve cut into
big squares, warm or cold, with a green
salad.

• Per serving 426 kcalories, protein 7g, carbohydrate
31g, fat 31g, saturated fat 13g, fibre 2g, added sugar
none, salt 0.58g

This couldn't be simpler – just arrange the topping
in neat rows on ready-rolled puff pastry.

Brie and Tomato Tart

250g/9oz puff pastry
225g/8oz brie
4–5 largish ripe tomatoes
225g/8oz courgettes
½ tsp dried oregano

Takes 45 minutes • Serves 4

1 Preheat the oven to 200°C/Gas 6/fan oven 180°C. Roll out the pastry to a 23 × 30cm/9 × 12in oblong, put on a damp baking sheet, and score the pastry with a knife 2.5cm/1in from the edges. Prick the base with a fork, inside the marks.
2 Slice the brie, tomatoes and courgettes into thin slices. Heat two tablespoons of olive oil in a frying pan and fry the courgettes for 1–2 minutes until softened. Add the oregano; season. Cook for 1–2 minutes; cool slightly.
3 Starting from one short end, arrange four overlapping rows of Brie, tomatoes and courgettes within the cut marks. Drizzle over the pan juices; season. Bake for 25–30 minutes until the pastry is puffed up and the courgettes are tender. Serve warm.

• Per serving 419 kcalories, protein 15g, carbohydrate 27g, fat 29g, saturated fat 9g, fibre 2g, added sugar none, salt 1.41g

The big mushrooms cook to a moist firmness under their cloak of peppers and melting goat's cheese.

Stuffed Mushroom Bruschettas

4 thick slices country-style loaf, white or brown
2 × 20g tubs garlic butter or 50g/ 2oz softened butter beaten with 1 chopped garlic clove
4 large flat mushrooms
olive oil, for drizzling
200g jar roasted red peppers, either strips in oil or whole peppers in brine
140g/5oz firm goat's cheese
mixed salad, to serve

Takes 40 minutes • Serves 2

1 Preheat the oven to 190°C/Gas 5/fan oven 170°C. Spread both sides of each slice of bread with garlic butter (no need to remove the crusts). Put the bread slices in one layer on a baking sheet.
2 Put a mushroom on top of each and drizzle with a little olive oil. Season. Drain the peppers, slice if necessary, and divide between the mushrooms.
3 Cut the goat's cheese into four slices and put one slice on top of each stack. Bake for 25–30 minutes, until the mushrooms are cooked and the cheese golden. Serve with a mixed salad.

• Per serving 679 kcalories, protein 27g, carbohydrate 45g, fat 45g, saturated fat 27g, fibre 5g, added sugar none, salt 2.9g

This dish is perfect for easy entertaining
on nights at home with friends.

Cheese and Chutney Melts

4 large crusty bread rolls
2 tbsp olive oil
4 tbsp green tomato chutney
4 small, rinded goat's cheeses
4 sprigs thyme
green salad, to serve (optional)

Takes 30 minutes • Serves 4

1 Preheat the oven to 190°C/Gas 5/fan oven 170°C. Cut a deep hollow in the top of each roll. Remove the bread from the centre and brush the insides with the oil. Season. Place on a baking sheet and bake for 5 minutes until lightly crisped.

2 Spoon the chutney into the rolls. Remove the rind from the top and bottom of each cheese and place one in each of the rolls. Push a sprig of thyme into the top and season with black pepper.

3 Scrunch foil around the roll, leaving the cheese uncovered. Bake for 15–20 minutes, until the cheese is golden and bubbling, removing the foil for the last 5 minutes. Serve with a green salad, if liked.

• Per serving 399 kcalories, protein 15g, carbohydrate 45g, fat 19g, saturated fat 7g, fibre 1g, added sugar 3g, salt 1.68g

Remember that the mushrooms shrink during cooking.
You could use medium mushrooms and serve more.

Herby Stuffed Mushrooms

4 very large flat mushrooms
2 tbsp olive oil

FOR THE STUFFING
3 sprigs fresh thyme
4 tbsp chopped fresh flatleaf parsley
100g/4oz roasted, shelled pistachio nuts, chopped
85g/3oz pitted black olives, chopped
finely grated zest and juice of ½ lemon
100g/4oz white breadcrumbs
140g/5oz feta, cut into small cubes
crusty bread, to serve
green salad, to serve (optional)

Takes 30 minutes • Serves 4

1 Preheat the oven to 200°C/Gas 6/fan oven 180°C. Remove the mushroom stalks and chop roughly. Brush the mushrooms with a little olive oil. Place in a roasting tin and season. Bake for 10 minutes until beginning to soften.
2 Meanwhile, mix all the stuffing ingredients with the chopped mushroom stalks and the remaining olive oil. Season.
3 Spoon the stuffing on top of the mushrooms and bake for a further 5–8 minutes, until the feta begins to soften. Serve immediately on toasted crusty bread with a green salad, if liked.

• Per serving 433 kcalories, protein 15g, carbohydrate 24g, fat 31g, saturated fat 8g, fibre 2g, added sugar none, salt 2.96g

Ready-made polenta is sold in large sausage or oblong shapes.
Not to be confused with quick-cook polenta powder.

Pizza-topped Polenta

500g pack ready-made polenta
½ tsp dried oregano
25g/1oz freshly grated parmesan
50g/2oz cheddar, grated
4 tbsp olive oil
4 large flat mushrooms,
stalks removed
400g/14oz ripe tomatoes,
roughly chopped
1 garlic clove, finely chopped

Takes 55 minutes • Serves 4

1 Preheat the oven to 220°C/Gas 7/fan oven 200°C from cold. Cut the polenta into 12 slices, 1cm/½in thick, and lay in four overlapping piles in a roasting tin. Sprinkle with oregano and most of the cheese. Pour the oil in a bowl, season and brush each mushroom. Place stalk-side up on the polenta piles.
2 Tip the tomatoes and garlic into the remaining oil. Spoon the tomatoes and their juices in and around the mushrooms and polenta, then season.
3 Sprinkle over the remaining cheese. Roast for 30 minutes until the tomatoes have softened and the mushrooms are tender. Serve hot.

• Per serving 422 kcalories, protein 14g, carbohydrate 50g, fat 20g, saturated fat 6g, fibre 3g, added sugar none, salt 0.42g

Halloumi cheese can be toasted in a pan without much oil –
softening the cheese rather than melting it.

Halloumi Vegetable Pan Fry

3 tbsp olive oil
250g/9oz halloumi, cut into slices
2 medium onions, cut in wedges
3 courgettes, sliced
8 tomatoes, halved
420g can butter beans, drained

Takes 30 minutes • Serves 4

1 Heat two tablespoons of the oil in a roasting tin or large frying pan, add the halloumi slices and fry until golden on both sides. Lift out, cut each slice into quarters and set aside. Add the onions to the tin and fry for 5 minutes until golden.
2 Toss in the courgettes and fry until golden. Remove the onions and courgettes from the tin and set aside. Heat the remaining oil in the tin and fry the tomatoes until softened and juicy.
3 Return the onions, courgettes and halloumi to the tin with the beans. Warm through, gently tossing it all together as you go. Season and serve.

• Per serving 285 kcalories, protein 20g, carbohydrate 29g, fat 22g, saturated fat 9g, fibre 8g, added sugar none, salt 2.35g

Polenta slices are also good cooked on a hot,
oiled griddle, turned once, until pleasantly charred.

Polenta Dolcelatte Grill

500g/1lb 2oz ready-made polenta,
thickly sliced
2 tbsp olive oil
3 plum tomatoes, cut into wedges
140g/5oz dolcelatte, cubed
6 tbsp chilli jam
green beans, to serve

Takes 45 minutes • Serves 4

1 Preheat the grill to high. Place the polenta slices on the grill pan, brush with olive oil and season well. Grill for 10–15 minutes, until lightly charred. Turn over, brush with oil and grill for a further 10 minutes.

2 Arrange the polenta and tomato wedges in a 2 litre/3½ pint shallow, heatproof dish, drizzle over the remaining olive oil. Grill for 5–10 minutes until the tomatoes soften. Top with the dolcelatte. Grill for 2–3 minutes until melted.

3 Meanwhile, place the chilli jam in a small pan and heat gently for 1–2 minutes. Place the grilled polenta, cheese and tomatoes on a plate with a spoonful of the chilli jam. Serve with green beans.

• Per serving 523 kcalories, protein 16g, carbohydrate 59g, fat 27g, saturated fat 10g, fibre 2g, added sugar none, salt 3.55g

Couscous just needs soaking, so it's the
perfect accompaniment to a speedy pan fry.

Halloumi and Pepper Couscous

150g/5½oz couscous
290g jar mixed pepper antipasti
2 tbsp olive oil
1 garlic clove, crushed
140g/5oz mixed mushrooms, sliced
140g/5oz halloumi, cubed
15g/½oz mixed fresh herbs (oregano,
basil, flatleaf parsley), finely
chopped, plus extra, to garnish

Takes 15 minutes • Serves 2

1 Place the couscous in a shallow dish and
pour over 300ml/½ pint boiling water. Cover
tightly with cling film and leave for 5 minutes.
Meanwhile, pour the antipasti into a small
pan and heat gently for 3–4 minutes.
2 Heat one tablespoon of the olive oil in
a large frying pan and fry the garlic for
1 minute. Add the mushrooms and fry for
3–4 minutes until lightly golden. Set aside.
Meanwhile, add the remaining olive oil to the
frying pan and fry the halloumi for 2 minutes
until lightly golden.
3 Stir the antipasti and chopped herbs
through the couscous and season. Spoon
on to plates and top with the pan-fried
halloumi and mushrooms. Garnish with
the extra herbs and serve.

• Per serving 695 kcalories, protein 29g, carbohydrate
48g, fat 44g, saturated fat 17g, fibre 4g, added sugar
none, salt 0.94g

A simple but filling supper speeded up
with help from the microwave.

Cheesy Bread Pudding

25g/1oz butter, softened
6 slices white bread (day-old bread
is best)
4 medium eggs, beaten
100ml/3½oz milk
50g/2oz vegetarian parmesan,
finely grated
1 tbsp Dijon mustard
25g/1oz vegetarian cheddar, grated
tomato and spring onion salad,
to serve

Takes 25 minutes • Serves 4

1 Spread the butter on one side of each slice of bread and cut into triangles. Arrange in a 1.5 litre/2¾ pint microwaveproof dish.
2 In a bowl, mix together the eggs, milk, parmesan and mustard and pour over the bread. Leave to stand for 5 minutes. Preheat the grill to hot. Microwave the pudding on High for 5 minutes.
3 Sprinkle over the cheddar and grill for 2–3 minutes until golden. Serve hot with a tomato and spring onion salad.

• Per serving 312 kcalories, protein 17g, carbohydrate 20g, fat 19g, saturated fat 9g, fibre 1g, added sugar none, salt 1.56g

This tart can stretch to feed extra people,
with a big mixed salad and garlic bread.

Stilton and Walnut Tart

600g/1lb 5oz onions
1 tbsp balsamic vinegar
375g pack ready-rolled puff pastry
175g/6oz stilton
50g pack walnut pieces

Takes 45 minutes • Serves 6

1 Preheat the oven to 200°C/Gas 6/fan oven 180°C. Peel the onions and thinly slice them. Heat three tablespoons of olive oil in a large frying pan, add the onions and fry until softened and lightly browned, stirring occasionally. This will take about 10 minutes.

2 Splash in the vinegar, season, then cook for a further 5 minutes, until lightly caramelised. Leave to cool while you prepare the pastry. Unroll the pastry and use to line a 23 × 33cm/9 × 13in shallow oblong tin.

3 Spread over the onions, then crumble the stilton on top and scatter with walnuts. Bake for 15–20 minutes, until the pastry is crisp and golden and the cheese has melted. Cool for 5 minutes before serving, cut into squares.

• Per serving 446 kcalories, protein 13g, carbohydrate 31g, fat 31g, saturated fat 7g, fibre 2g, added sugar none, salt 1.19g

Quick and tasty and cooked in one pan so there's hardly any washing up.

Spaghetti Genovese

300g/10oz new potatoes, sliced
300g/10oz spaghetti
225g/8oz trimmed green beans,
cut in half
120g carton fresh pesto
olive oil, for drizzling

Takes 20 minutes • Serves 4

1 Pour boiling water into a very large pan until half full. Return to the boil, then add the potatoes and spaghetti, and a little salt.
2 Cook for 10 minutes until the potatoes and pasta are almost tender. Tip in the green beans and cook for 5 minutes more.
3 Drain well, reserving four tablespoons of the cooking liquid. Return the potatoes, pasta and beans to the pan, then stir in the fresh pesto and reserved cooking liquid. Season to taste, divide between four serving plates and drizzle with a little olive oil.

• Per serving 330 kcalories, protein 23g, carbohydrate 8g, fat 23g, saturated fat 9g, fibre trace, added sugar 7g, salt 0.5g

A simple sauce based on a can of beans from the storecupboard,
plus wine and cream for richness.

Pasta with Flageolet Beans

2 tbsp olive oil
2 small red onions, cut into
thick wedges
4 garlic cloves, roughly chopped
400g can flageolet beans,
drained and rinsed
1 tbsp chopped fresh rosemary
150ml/¼ pint vegetable stock
150ml/¼ pint white wine
4 tbsp double cream
100g/4oz green beans
350g/12oz pappardelle (broad
pasta ribbons)

Takes 40 minutes • Serves 4

1 Heat the oil in large pan, add the onions and cook until softened. Add the garlic, flageolet beans, rosemary, stock and wine and simmer for 10 minutes.
2 Season, add the cream and simmer for a further 5 minutes. Meanwhile, bring a pan of lightly salted water to the boil. Add the green beans and cook for 5 minutes until tender. Remove with a slotted spoon and keep hot.
3 Add the pasta to the boiling water and cook according to the packet instructions. Drain and toss with the creamy sauce. Divide between four bowls and serve topped with the green beans.

• Per serving 582 kcalories, protein 21g, carbohydrate 85g, fat 18g, saturated fat 6g, fibre 9g, added sugar none, salt 0.95g

Egg yolks and cream make one of the quickest
and most delicious pasta sauces.

Spaghetti Carbonara

350g/12oz tricolour spaghetti
225g/8oz baby carrots,
halved lengthways
fine asparagus, sliced into
3cm/1¼in lengths
1 large courgette, cut into ribbons
2 medium egg yolks
200ml/7fl oz double cream
50g/2oz vegetarian
parmesan, grated
50g/2oz sun-dried tomatoes in oil,
drained and sliced

Takes 25 minutes • Serves 4

1 Cook the pasta in a large pan of lightly salted boiling water according to the packet instructions. About 4 minutes before the end of cooking add the carrots.
2 After 2 minutes add the asparagus and just before draining stir in the courgette ribbons. Drain and return to the pan over a low heat. Beat together the egg yolks, cream and half the parmesan and season well.
3 Pour over the pasta and vegetables and heat very gently for 2–3 minutes, stirring constantly, until the sauce has thickened slightly – do not overheat or the eggs will scramble. Stir in the sun-dried tomatoes and serve with the remaining parmesan and plenty of black pepper.

• Per serving 651 kcalories, protein 20g, carbohydrate 71g, fat 34g, saturated fat 19g, fibre 5g, added sugar none, salt 0.51g

Chilli, lemon, pine nuts and sultanas make
bland pasta and cauliflower surprisingly tasty.

Spicy Cauliflower Pasta

1 medium cauliflower,
cut into small florets
350g/12oz trompetti or other
pasta tubes
4 tbsp olive oil
2 garlic cloves, sliced
1 red chilli, seeded and sliced
85g/3oz pine nuts
50g/2oz sultanas
finely pared zest of 1 lemon,
shredded (or use a zester)
juice of ½ lemon
4 tbsp chopped fresh parsley
50g/2oz vegetarian parmesan,
grated (optional)

Takes 20 minutes • Serves 4

1 Cook the cauliflower in salted boiling
water for 2 minutes. Drain and rinse with
cold water to stop it cooking further. Drain.
Cook the pasta in salted boiling water
according to the packet instructions.
2 Meanwhile, heat the oil in a large frying
pan. Add the cauliflower and fry for 3 minutes
until lightly golden. Reduce the heat, add the
garlic, chilli and pine nuts and cook for a
further 2 minutes.
3 Add the drained pasta, the sultanas,
lemon zest and juice and parsley. Season
and toss together with the parmesan, if
using.

• Per serving 691 kcalories, protein 22g, carbohydrate
78g, fat 35g, saturated fat 6g, fibre 5g, added sugar
none, salt 0.42g

Taleggio is a small rectangular Italian
cheese that melts wonderfully over pasta.

Pasta with Taleggio

2 tbsp olive oil
1 onion, sliced
1 red, 1 yellow and 1 green pepper,
seeded and sliced
2 garlic cloves, sliced
300ml/½ pint passata
(sieved tomatoes)
350g/12oz rigatoni (ridged
pasta tubes)
pinch of sugar (optional)
handful of fresh basil, torn
250g/9oz taleggio cheese,
thinly sliced

Takes 45 minutes • Serves 4

1 Heat the oil in a large frying pan and fry the onion for 2–3 minutes. Add the peppers and cook over a medium heat until lightly browned. Reduce the heat, add the garlic, and cook for 2 minutes. Stir in the passata and 150ml/¼ pint water. Bring to the boil and simmer for 15 minutes until the sauce is thickened and reduced.

2 Meanwhile, cook the pasta in salted boiling water according to the packet instructions. Preheat the grill to high. Season the sauce and add a pinch of sugar, if necessary. Add the drained pasta and half the basil and spread into a shallow, flameproof dish.

3 Arrange the cheese over the top and grill for 5 minutes until the cheese is melted. Scatter over the remaining basil and serve.

• Per serving 692 kcalories, protein 15g, carbohydrate 75g, fat 39g, saturated fat 20g, fibre 5g, added sugar 15g, salt 0.59g

Pumpkin can be bland but here it's spiced up with chilli, sage and lemon zest.

Ravioli with Pumpkin

500g/1lb 2oz packet fresh cheese ravioli
1 tbsp olive oil
1 onion, finely chopped
1 garlic clove, crushed
425g can solid pumpkin
50g/2oz vegetarian parmesan, finely grated
pinch of crushed chilli flakes
finely grated zest of 1 lemon
25g/1oz butter
85g/3oz fresh white breadcrumbs
2 tbsp chopped fresh sage
deep-fried sage leaves, to garnish (optional)

Takes 30 minutes • Serves 4

1 Cook the ravioli according to the packet instructions. Meanwhile, heat the olive oil in a small pan and fry the onion and garlic for 2–3 minutes, until softened. Add the pumpkin, 300ml/½ pint water, the grated parmesan, chilli flakes and lemon zest. Stir well and cook over a low heat for 3–4 minutes. Season.
2 In a small frying pan, melt the butter, then stir in the breadcrumbs and fry until lightly golden. Stir in the chopped sage.
3 Drain the ravioli and spoon into bowls. Pour over the pumpkin sauce and sprinkle with the toasted sage breadcrumbs. Serve with the deep-fried sage, if liked.

• Per serving 674 kcalories, protein 26g, carbohydrate 94g, fat 24g, saturated fat 12g, fibre 5g, added sugar none, salt 1.28g

Don't bother with layering the lasagne in a dish,
this easy version is assembled on the plate.

Chilli Bean Open Lasagne

1 tbsp olive oil
1 onion, chopped
2 garlic cloves, crushed
1 red chilli, finely sliced
1 small aubergine, chopped
1 large courgette, chopped
410g can borlotti beans, drained
400g can chopped tomatoes
2 tbsp tomato purée
250g pack fresh lasagne sheets
handful of basil, torn
100g/4oz vegetarian
cheddar, grated
green salad, to serve

Takes 30 minutes • Serves 4

1 Heat the oil in a large frying pan. Fry the onion for 3 minutes, until softened. Add the garlic, chilli, aubergine and courgette and fry for a further 2 minutes. Stir in the beans, tomatoes and tomato purée and season. Bring to the boil and simmer for 5 minutes.
2 Meanwhile, cook the lasagne sheets in salted boiling water according to the packet instructions. Drain, then halve each sheet diagonally. Stir all but four of the basil sprigs into the bean mixture.
3 Place a spoonful of the mixture on to each plate and top with a quarter of the lasagne triangles. Top with the remaining bean mix, grated cheese and the basil sprigs. Serve with a green salad.

• Per serving 400 kcalories, protein 17g, carbohydrate 73g, fat 6g, saturated fat 1g, fibre 11g, added sugar none, salt 1.21g

Using fresh pasta in this dish means there's
no pre-cooking needed.

Cheese and Tomato Cannelloni

5 tbsp fruity olive oil
750g/1lb 10oz ripe cherry tomatoes
2 tsp dried oregano
2 tsp golden caster sugar
6 tbsp fresh red or green pesto
225g/8oz soft rindless goat's cheese
12 fresh lasagne sheets
350g/12oz ripe vine tomatoes,
thinly sliced
3 tbsp freshly grated parmesan
basil leaves and green salad,
to serve

Takes 1 hour 20 minutes • Serves 4

1 Preheat the oven to 220°C/Gas 7/fan oven 200°C. Oil a shallow baking dish. Halve 250g/9oz of the cherry tomatoes. Heat the oil in a frying pan, add the whole cherry tomatoes, cover and cook over a high heat, shaking the pan, for 5 minutes. Add the oregano and sugar. Season.
2 Beat the pesto into the goat's cheese. Lay out the lasagne and spread the cheese mixture over each sheet. Top with tomato slices and roll up like a Swiss roll. Spoon half the cherry tomato sauce into the dish. Arrange the pasta rolls on top and spoon over any remaining tomato sauce. Scatter the cherry tomato halves on top and cover with foil.
3 Bake for 25–30 minutes. Uncover, sprinkle with the cheese and bake for 10 minutes until brown. Serve with basil and a green salad.

• Per serving 635 kcalories, protein 21g, carbohydrate 57g, fat 37g, saturated fat 5g, fibre 6g, added sugar 3g, salt 1.46g

This pasta dish is perfect to have bubbling in
the oven while you chat to your guests.

Fiorentina Baked Pasta

1 tbsp olive oil
500g/1lb 2oz chestnut
mushrooms, halved
2 garlic cloves, chopped
300g carton fresh spinach and
cheese sauce
300ml/½ pint milk
50g/2oz vegetarian parmesan
cheese, grated
300g/10oz puntalette
(rice-shaped pasta)

Takes 1 hour • Serves 4

1 Preheat the oven to 190°C/Gas 5/fan oven 170°C. Heat the oil in a large frying pan, add the mushrooms and cook over a high heat for 5 minutes until lightly golden. Reduce the heat, add the garlic and cook for 2 minutes. Season and place in a shallow 1.5 litre/2¾ pint ovenproof dish.

2 Place the spinach sauce, milk, half the parmesan and pasta in a large bowl. Stir and season to taste. Pour over the mushrooms and scatter over the remaining parmesan.

3 Bake for 45 minutes until the pasta is tender and most of the liquid has been absorbed.

• Per serving 594 kcalories, protein 27g, carbohydrate 67g, fat 26g, saturated fat 12g, fibre 4g, added sugar none, salt 1.56g

Gnocchi are small Italian dumplings,
treated like pasta and served with a tasty sauce.

Lemon Butter Gnocchi

400g packet fresh potato gnocchi
2 tbsp olive oil
300g/10oz butternut squash,
peeled, halved, seeded
and roughly chopped
1 tsp sugar
finely grated zest of 1 lemon and
½ of the juice
85g/3oz butter
2 tbsp chopped fresh rosemary
green salad, to serve

Takes 20 minutes • Serves 2

1 Cook the gnocchi according to the packet instructions. Meanwhile, heat the oil in a small frying pan and fry the butternut squash for 5 minutes until tender. Sprinkle over the sugar and lemon zest and fry for a further minute until slightly caramelised.

2 Melt the butter in a small pan. Stir in the lemon juice and chopped rosemary and season to taste. Drain the gnocchi and stir into the butternut squash. Stir well to combine.

3 Spoon into warmed serving bowls, then drizzle the lemon and rosemary butter sauce over. Serve with a green salad.

• Per serving 615 kcalories, protein 8g, carbohydrate 63g, fat 39g, saturated fat 21g, fibre 5g, added sugar 3g, salt 0.97g

Potato gnocchi, bought vacuum-packed, make
a great fridge or freezer stand-by.

Gnocchi with Broad Beans

350g packet potato gnocchi
2 tbsp olive oil
250g/9oz small cup
mushrooms, halved
2 garlic cloves, crushed
225g/8oz frozen baby broad beans
3 tbsp chopped fresh tarragon
250g mascarpone cheese
1 tbsp lemon juice
vegetarian parmesan shavings and
pared lemon zest, to garnish
salad, to serve (optional)

Takes 20 minutes • Serves 4

1 Cook the gnocchi according to the packet instructions. Drain and set aside. Heat the oil in a frying pan, add the mushrooms and fry quickly over a high heat until browned. Lift out with a slotted spoon and add to the gnocchi.

2 Wipe out the pan then add the garlic, beans, tarragon and mascarpone. Heat gently, stirring, until the mascarpone has melted. Add the lemon juice, mushrooms and gnocchi to the frying pan. Heat through for 1 minute. Season to taste.

3 Divide between serving plates and scatter over the parmesan shavings and pared lemon zest. Serve with salad leaves, if liked.

• Per serving 488 kcalories, protein 10g, carbohydrate 28g, fat 38g, saturated fat 20g, fibre 5g, added sugar none, salt 0.54g

This version is cooked in the microwave,
which cuts down the need for stirring.

Leek and Mushroom Risotto

25g/1oz butter
1 tbsp olive oil
1 leek, cut into thin slices
1 garlic clove, crushed
300g/10oz risotto rice
850ml/1½ pints hot vegetable stock
250g/9oz chestnut
mushrooms, sliced
50g/2oz fresh parmesan, grated
green salad, to serve

Takes 40 minutes • Serves 4

1 Put the butter, oil, leek and garlic into a large bowl. Cover with cling film and cook on High for 5 minutes.
2 Stir the rice into the hot leeks, then stir in the stock and season. Cook, uncovered, on High for 10 minutes. Throw in the mushrooms, stir and cook on High for 6 minutes.
3 Mix in half the parmesan and leave the risotto to stand for 5 minutes. Serve with a green salad and the remaining parmesan for sprinkling.

• Per serving 397 kcalories, protein 13g, carbohydrate 60g, fat 13g, saturated fat 6g, fibre 3g, added sugar none, salt 1.22g

This oven-baked risotto works beautifully and saves effort as you don't have to stand over it.

Baked Spinach Risotto

25g/1oz butter
1 garlic clove, crushed
1 small red onion, chopped
100g/4oz risotto rice
1 tbsp chopped fresh rosemary, plus extra to garnish
300ml/½ pint vegetable stock
250ml/9fl oz white wine
290g jar antipasto mixed peppers in tomato dressing
50g/2oz spinach
25g/1oz vegetarian parmesan, grated
green salad, to serve

Takes 55 minutes • Serves 2

1 Preheat the oven to 180°C/Gas 4/fan oven 160°C. Put the butter and garlic in a 1 litre/1¾ pint ovenproof dish and place in the oven for 2 minutes until the butter has melted. Add the onion and toss to coat in the butter, then return to the oven for a further 3–4 minutes to soften.
2 Add the rice, rosemary, stock and wine and return to the oven for 30 minutes, stirring once or twice during cooking.
3 Stir in the antipasto peppers and spinach and return to the oven for another 10 minutes, until all the liquid has been absorbed. Stir in the parmesan and season to taste. Serve with a fresh green salad.

• Per serving 534 kcalories, protein 11g, carbohydrate 54g, fat 23g, saturated fat 10g, fibre 3g, added sugar none, salt 1.25g

A simple dish, easily varied by adding peas,
fried mushrooms or sweetcorn.

Cheddar and Tomato Rice

2 tbsp oil
1 onion, thinly sliced
1 red pepper, cored, seeded
and sliced
1 garlic clove, finely chopped
300g/10oz long grain rice
1 litre/1¾ pints vegetable stock
227g can chopped tomatoes
100g/4oz mature cheddar, cubed
chives and salad leaves, to garnish

Takes 1 hour • Serves 4

1 Preheat the oven to 180°C/Gas 4/fan oven 160°C from cold. Heat the oil in a large flameproof casserole, fry the onion and red pepper over a medium heat until golden. Add the chopped garlic and cook for a further minute.

2 Stir in the rice until completely coated in oil. Add the stock and tomatoes, and season. Bring to the boil and simmer for 5 minutes until nearly all the liquid has been absorbed.

3 Scatter over the cheese, cover the casserole and cook in the oven for about 30 minutes until the rice is tender. Leave for 5 minutes before garnishing with chives and salad leaves.

• Per serving 463 kcalories, protein 14g, carbohydrate 72g, fat 15g, saturated fat 6g, fibre 2g, added sugar none, salt 1.32g

Cook the rice earlier in the day because it
stir fries better when it's cooled first.

Thai Fried Rice with Vegetables

2 tbsp sunflower oil
1 red chilli, finely sliced
1 stalk lemongrass, finely chopped
2 shallots, finely sliced
1 garlic clove, crushed
5cm/2in piece fresh root ginger,
finely chopped
140g/5oz jasmine rice, cooked
and cooled
1 small red pepper, seeded
and sliced
1 carrot, cut into matchsticks
2 spring onions, shredded
85g/3oz mangetout, sliced
1 tbsp light soy sauce
25g/1oz coconut shavings, toasted
fresh coriander leaves

Takes 35 minutes • Serves 2

1 Heat one tablespoon of the oil in a wok or large frying pan. Stir fry the chilli, lemongrass, shallots, garlic and ginger over a low heat for 2 minutes until softened. Add the cooked rice and fry, stirring, for a further 3–4 minutes.
2 Meanwhile, heat the remaining oil in another frying pan and toss in the pepper, carrot, spring onions and mangetout. Stir fry for 2–3 minutes.
3 Stir the soy sauce into the rice and spoon into serving bowls. Top with the vegetables, coconut shavings and torn coriander leaves and serve.

• Per serving 930 kcalories, protein 17g, carbohydrate 177g, fat 22g, saturated fat 6g, fibre 5g, added sugar none, salt 1.17g

You could use leftover rice to make this tasty and colourful Indonesian fried rice mixture, if it has been kept well chilled.

Spicy Nasi Goreng

300g/10oz long grain rice, rinsed
2 medium eggs, beaten
3 garlic cloves
2 red chillies, thinly sliced
2 onions, sliced
3 tbsp groundnut oil
1 yellow pepper, seeded and sliced
2 carrots, cut into matchsticks
2 tbsp dark soy sauce
4 spring onions, shredded
4 tbsp chopped fresh coriander

Takes 35 minutes • Serves 2

1 Place the rice in a wok, add 600ml/1 pint water and bring to the boil. Cover and cook over a very low heat for 15 minutes, until all the liquid has been absorbed. Tip into a shallow dish and leave to cool.

2 Meanwhile, heat the wok. Add the eggs and cook, stirring, until scrambled. Remove and set aside. Whizz the garlic, half the chilli and half the onion to a paste in a blender. Heat the oil in the wok and fry the paste for 1 minute. Add the rest of the onion and chilli, plus the vegetables and stir fry for 2 minutes.

3 Add the cold rice and stir fry for 3 minutes. Stir in the soy sauce, spring onions and eggs and fry until piping hot. Season and serve immediately.

• Per serving 445 kcalories, protein 10g, carbohydrate 72g, fat 15g, saturated fat 3g, fibre 2g, added sugar none, salt 0.16g

A pack of egg noodles is a useful storecupboard item. They cook quickly and are good with stir fries as well as in a warm salad.

Sesame Noodle Salad

140g pack medium egg noodles
3 tbsp sesame oil
1 tbsp dark soy sauce
2 tsp lemon juice
1 large carrot, peeled
10cm/4in piece cucumber
or courgette
2 tsp sesame seeds
2 garlic cloves, finely chopped
25g/1oz fresh root ginger, peeled
and finely chopped
4 spring onions, shredded
½–1 tsp Chinese five-spice powder
handful of lamb's lettuce or rocket

Takes 15 minutes • Serves 2

1 Cook the noodles according to the packet instructions. Rinse in a colander under cold water and drain well. Tip into a bowl and add the sesame oil, soy sauce and lemon juice.
2 Use a potato peeler to cut the carrot into fine ribbons. Do the same with the cucumber or courgette, discarding the central seed section. Add to the noodles.
3 Heat a small pan and dry fry the sesame seeds until pale golden. Sprinkle over the noodles. Add the oil to the pan and stir fry the garlic, ginger, spring onions and five-spice powder for 30 seconds. Stir in the lettuce or rocket leaves. Toss with the noodles, season and serve.

• Per serving 655 kcalories, protein 15g, carbohydrate 58g, fat 42g, saturated fat 5g, fibre 6g, added sugar none, salt 1.47g

Tofu is bean curd. It tastes bland but, like chicken,
it is good at absorbing flavours from other ingredients.

Tofu Chow Mein

250g egg noodles
1 tbsp vegetable oil
3 spring onions, sliced
2 garlic cloves, finely chopped
2cm/¾in piece fresh root ginger,
peeled and finely chopped
285g pack firm tofu,
cut into small cubes
227g can bamboo shoots, sliced
100g/4oz beansprouts
100g/4oz mangetout,
sliced lengthways
2 tbsp soy sauce
2 tbsp sweet chilli sauce

Takes 25 minutes • Serves 4

1 Cook the noodles according to the packet instructions. Meanwhile, heat the oil in a large frying pan or wok and stir fry the spring onions, garlic and ginger for 1–2 minutes, until slightly softened.

2 Add the tofu cubes and fry over a high heat for 2–3 minutes until golden. Stir in the bamboo shoots, beansprouts and mangetout and stir fry for a further 1–2 minutes.

3 Drain the noodles and add to the vegetables with the soy sauce and chilli sauce. Toss together and serve immediately.

• Per serving 361 kcalories, protein 16g, carbohydrate 49g, fat 12g, saturated fat 1g, fibre 4g, added sugar none, salt 1.4g

Look out for pre-cooked, vacuum-packed noodles that can be added straight to the wok without pre-boiling.

Thai Satay Noodles

3 tbsp crunchy peanut butter
3 tbsp sweet chilli sauce
100ml/3½fl oz thick coconut milk
100ml/3½fl oz vegetable stock
2 tbsp soy sauce
300g pack pre-cooked, vacuum-packed thin egg noodles
2 tbsp sesame oil
5cm/2in piece fresh root ginger, grated
140g/5oz broccoli florets
1 small red pepper, seeded and sliced
85g/3oz baby corn, halved lengthways
50g/2oz mangetout
3 garlic cloves, finely chopped
small handful fresh basil leaves
25g/1oz roasted peanuts, roughly chopped

Takes 25 minutes • Serves 4

1 Mix the peanut butter, chilli sauce, coconut milk, stock and soy sauce to make a smooth satay sauce. Pour boiling water over the noodles and stir gently to separate them.
2 Heat the oil in a wok and stir fry the ginger, broccoli, peppers and corn for 3 minutes. Add the mangetout and garlic and stir fry for a further 2 minutes. Pour over the peanut sauce and bring to the boil.
3 Drain the noodles thoroughly. Add to the wok and stir fry over a high heat for 1–2 minutes. Sprinkle over the basil leaves and peanuts and serve.

• Per serving 588 kcalories, protein 18g, carbohydrate 62g, fat 31g, saturated fat 8g, fibre 7g, added sugar none, salt 1.8g

Use tangy, half-fat crème fraîche or soured
cream if you are unable to get hold of smetana.

Roast Beetroot with Horseradish

1kg/2lb 4oz fresh, uncooked
beetroot, peeled and
cut into wedges
400g/14oz shallots, halved if large
3 tbsp olive oil
3 tbsp balsamic vinegar
3 tsp caraway seeds, plus extra
for sprinkling
plain boiled rice, to serve
handful of fresh chives, to garnish

FOR THE SAUCE
150ml/¼ pint smetana
25g/1oz fresh horseradish, grated,
or 2 tbsp hot horseradish
from a jar

Takes 1 hour • Serves 4

1 Preheat the oven to 200°C/Gas 6/fan
oven 180°C. Place the beetroot in a large
roasting tin along with the shallots. Drizzle
over the olive oil and balsamic vinegar,
season and toss well to coat. Roast for
25 minutes.
2 Add the caraway seeds to the tin and
toss together. Roast for a further 20 minutes,
until the beetroot is tender and the shallots
are softened and golden.
3 Mix together the smetana and
horseradish and season. Serve the roasted
vegetables with plain boiled rice. Spoon
over the smetana mixture and garnish with
the caraway seeds and fresh chives.

• Per serving 256 kcalories, protein 9g, carbohydrate
28g, fat 13g, saturated fat 2g, fibre 7g, added sugar
none, salt 0.53g

Quick-cook polenta is a great midweek standby.
Quark is a piquant cow's milk curd cheese.

Spring Vegetable Polenta

FOR THE POLENTA
850ml/1½ pints vegetable stock
175g/6oz quick-cook polenta
100g/4oz quark
125g jar vegetarian pesto sauce
vegetarian parmesan shavings,
to serve (optional)

FOR THE VEGETABLES
100g/4oz baby corn,
halved lengthways
100g/4oz baby carrots, trimmed
100g/4oz flat or runner beans,
trimmed and thickly sliced
100g/4oz fresh (or frozen) peas
finely pared zest of
1 lemon, chopped
2 tbsp chopped fresh parsley
1 garlic clove, finely chopped

Takes 15 minutes • Serves 4

1 In a large pan, bring the stock to a rolling boil and shower in the polenta in a steady stream, whisking continuously, until thickened. Stir in the quark and cook over a low heat for a further 5 minutes, stirring occasionally.

2 Meanwhile, steam the vegetables over a pan of simmering water for 3–4 minutes. Remove the polenta from the heat and beat in the pesto sauce. Season to taste. Spoon on to warmed serving plates.

3 Serve the vegetables on top of the polenta. Scatter the lemon zest, parsley and garlic over and serve immediately with freshly shaved vegetarian parmesan, if liked.

• Per serving 394 kcalories, protein 15g, carbohydrate 40g, fat 21g, saturated fat 3g, fibre 4g, added sugar none, salt 1.27g

Serve this saucy curry in deep bowls with spoonfuls
of cooling fromage frais and warm bread for dunking.

Pumpkin and Apple Curry

1 tbsp sunflower oil
1 large onion, roughly chopped
3 garlic cloves, chopped
500g/1lb 2oz pumpkin, peeled,
seeded and cubed
800g/1lb 12oz baking
potatoes, cubed
1 medium cooking apple, peeled,
cored and diced
2 tsp mild curry paste
1 tsp turmeric
2.5cm/1in fresh root
ginger, chopped
2 bay leaves
1 vegetable stock cube
50g/2oz raisins
4 tbsp fromage frais, to serve
bread or rice, to serve

Takes 45 minutes • Serves 4

1 Heat the oil in a pan, add the onion and
fry for 5 minutes until golden. Add the garlic,
pumpkin, potatoes and apple. Stir in the
curry paste, turmeric, ginger and bay leaves.
2 Add 500ml/18fl oz water, the stock cube,
raisins and plenty of seasoning. Bring to
the boil, stirring. Cover and simmer for
15 minutes, stirring occasionally, until the
vegetables are tender.
3 Spoon into bowls and top with the
fromage frais and a pinch of turmeric.
Serve with bread or rice.

• Per serving 270 kcalories, protein 5g, carbohydrate
55g, fat 5g, saturated fat 1g, fibre 6g, added sugar
none, salt 0.23g

A filling tart, delicious served
hot or cold with salads.

Potato and Onion Tart

375g pack ready-rolled shortcrust
pastry, thawed if frozen
2 tbsp olive oil
450g/1lb onions, thinly sliced
2 garlic cloves, crushed
3 tbsp fresh thyme leaves or
1 tbsp dried
750g/1lb 10oz floury potatoes,
peeled and thickly sliced
2 eggs
200ml carton crème fraîche
2 tbsp wholegrain mustard
salad, to serve

Takes 50 minutes • Serves 4

1 Preheat the oven to 220°C/Gas 7/fan
oven 200°C. Use the pastry to line the
base and sides of a Swiss roll tin about
23 × 33cm/9 × 13in. Heat the oil in a
large frying pan and fry the onions for
8–10 minutes, until just beginning to
caramelise. Stir in the garlic and most of
the thyme and cook for a further 2 minutes.
Scatter half into the pastry case.
2 Parboil the potatoes in salted boiling water
for 4–5 minutes. Drain well and arrange in the
case. Scatter over the remaining onions.
3 Beat together the eggs, crème fraîche
and mustard. Season well and pour over
the vegetables. Scatter over the rest of the
thyme and bake the tart for 20 minutes, until
the filling has set and is golden. Serve with
a salad.

• Per serving 706 kcalories, protein 14g, carbohydrate
84g, fat 37g, saturated fat 14g, fibre 6g, added sugar
none, salt 0.84g

A substantial main course salad with spiced canned
chickpeas and naan bread croûtons.

Indian Chickpea Salad

6 tbsp olive oil
3 garlic cloves, sliced
2 red chillies, seeded and sliced
4 tsp cumin seeds, lightly crushed
2 × 400g cans chickpeas, drained
and rinsed
3 tomatoes, halved, seeded
and diced
pared zest and juice of 1 lemon
1 naan bread

FOR THE SALAD
25g/1oz fresh coriander
½ cucumber, cut into batons
1 medium red onion, sliced
100g/4oz baby spinach leaves

Takes 30 minutes • Serves 4

1 Put five tablespoons of the oil in a pan.
Add the garlic, chillies and cumin and
warm over a medium heat for 10 minutes.
Take care not to burn the garlic. Add the
chickpeas and heat through for 5 minutes.
Meanwhile, preheat the grill to high.
2 Add the tomatoes, lemon zest and juice
to the chickpeas. Season and set aside.
Brush the naan bread with the remaining
oil and grill both sides until crisp. Tear into
bite-sized pieces.
3 Toss together the salad ingredients and
divide between serving plates. Spoon the
chickpeas over and top with the naan bread
croûtons.

• Per serving 641 kcalories, protein 23g, carbohydrate
66g, fat 33g, saturated fat 6g, fibre 11g, added sugar
0.2g, salt 0.65g

Couscous only needs to be soaked before you eat it,
so it's a useful accompaniment to colourful roasted vegetables.

Roasted Vegetable Couscous

1 each red and yellow pepper,
seeded and diced
2 courgettes, diced
1 aubergine, diced
1 red onion, chopped
2 garlic cloves, chopped
1 tbsp fresh rosemary, chopped
5 tbsp olive oil
250g/9oz couscous
400g can flageolet beans, drained
and rinsed
2 tbsp balsamic vinegar
green salad, to serve

Takes 45 minutes • Serves 4

1 Preheat the oven to 220°C/Gas 7/fan oven 200°C. Place all the vegetables, the garlic and rosemary in a large roasting tin and drizzle over four tablespoons oil. Season and roast for 20 minutes, stirring after 10 minutes.
2 Meanwhile, put the couscous in a bowl and pour over 400ml/14fl oz boiling water. Season and leave for 20 minutes until all the water has been absorbed. Add the flageolet beans and vinegar to the roasting tin, mix well and roast for a further 10 minutes.
3 Fluff up the couscous grains with a fork. Divide between serving plates and top with the roasted vegetable and bean mixture. Serve with a green salad.

• Per serving 478 kcalories, protein 15g, carbohydrate 61g, fat 21g, saturated fat 3g, fibre 7g, added sugar none, salt 0.06g

Most melting cheeses will taste great grilled on top of aubergine slices. Try using brie for a change.

Aubergines with Goat's Cheese

4 medium aubergines, halved lengthways
100ml/3½fl oz olive oil
2 tbsp sun-dried tomato paste
25g/1oz fresh basil leaves
4 × 60g individual, rinded goat's cheeses
1 tbsp white wine vinegar
1 tsp Dijon mustard
pinch of caster sugar
160g bag mixed salad leaves
85g/3oz radishes, halved
crusty bread, to serve

Takes 25 minutes • Serves 4

1 Preheat the grill to hot. Brush both sides of the aubergine halves with three tablespoons of the oil and season. Place the aubergines, cut-side up, on a baking sheet and grill for 7 minutes. Turn them over and grill for a further 5 minutes, until lightly scorched.
2 Spread the cut sides with the tomato paste and arrange basil leaves on top. Slice each cheese into four rounds and arrange on the aubergines. Season and grill until bubbling.
3 Whisk the remaining oil, vinegar, mustard and sugar in a salad bowl. Toss the vegetables in the dressing until coated. Divide between serving plates and arrange the cheesy aubergine halves on top. Serve with crusty bread.

• Per serving 416 kcalories, protein 12g, carbohydrate 10g, fat 37g, saturated fat 4g, fibre 7g, added sugar none, salt 2.36g

Paneer is a hard Indian cheese that melts deliciously into the sauce. Find it in supermarket chiller cabinets.

Pea and Paneer Curry

2 tbsp vegetable oil
227g pack paneer (Indian cheese), torn into pieces
1 onion, thinly sliced
2 tbsp mild curry paste
450g/1lb potatoes, peeled and cut into chunks
400g can chopped tomatoes with garlic
300ml/½ pint vegetable stock
300g/10oz frozen peas
boiled rice, to serve

Takes 45 minutes • Serves 4

1 Heat one tablespoon oil in a large saucepan. Fry the paneer for 2–3 minutes, stirring, until crisp and golden. Remove with a slotted spoon and set aside.

2 Fry the onion in the remaining oil for 4–5 minutes, until soft and just beginning to brown. Add the curry paste. Fry, stirring, for 2 minutes.

3 Add the potatoes, tomatoes, stock and paneer, bring to the boil and simmer for 15 minutes. Add the peas, bring to the boil and simmer for 5 minutes. Season to taste and serve with boiled rice.

• Per serving 404 kcalories, protein 20g, carbohydrate 32g, fat 22g, saturated fat 9g, fibre 7g, added sugar none, salt 2.84g

This is a really tasty supper dish and it's
easily doubled to feed those hungry hordes.

Tomato and Goat's Cheese Crumble

1kg/2lb 4oz ripe tomatoes,
preferably a mixture, including
a punnet of cherry tomatoes
5 tbsp olive oil
225g/8oz goat's cheese, firm or soft
50g/2oz pine nuts
100g/4oz fresh white breadcrumbs
50g/2oz parmesan, freshly grated
green salad or vegetables, to serve

Takes 55 minutes • Serves 4

1 Preheat the oven to 190°C/Gas 5/fan oven 170°C. Chop the tomatoes, keeping the cherry ones whole. Heat two tablespoons of olive oil in a pan, add the chopped tomatoes, season and cook for 10 minutes, until softened, stirring occasionally. Remove from the heat and stir in the cherry tomatoes.

2 Spoon half the tomatoes into a 1 litre/1¾ pint ovenproof dish and crumble half the goat's cheese on top. Repeat the layers.

3 Heat three tablespoons of olive oil in a frying pan and lightly fry the pine nuts and breadcrumbs. Remove from the heat and stir in half the parmesan. Scatter over the tomatoes and cheese and top with the remaining parmesan. Bake for 20–25 minutes, until golden. Serve with a green salad or vegetables.

• Per serving 431 kcalories, protein 22g, carbohydrate 28g, fat 27g, saturated fat 12g, fibre 3g, added sugar none, salt 1.78g

Instead of using bread dough, this pizza base is made from quick-cook polenta spread on a baking tray.

Polenta Pizza

250g pack quick-cook polenta
50g/2oz vegetarian parmesan, grated
1 tbsp olive oil
1 red onion, sliced
2 garlic cloves, sliced
1 courgette, sliced
100g/4oz chestnut mushrooms, sliced
4 ripe plum tomatoes, sliced
100g/4oz mozzarella, thinly sliced
1 tbsp vegetarian green pesto
green salad, to serve

Takes 50 minutes • Serves 4

1 Cook the polenta according to the packet instructions. Season well and stir in the parmesan. Pour on to an oiled baking sheet, spread out to a 28cm/11in circle and leave to firm up for 15 minutes. Meanwhile, preheat the oven to 200°C/Gas 6/fan oven 180°C.

2 Heat the oil in a large frying pan and fry the onion for 5 minutes, until softened. Add the garlic and courgettes and cook for a further 2 minutes. Season and scatter over the polenta base with the mushrooms and tomatoes.

3 Arrange the mozzarella on top and dot with the pesto. Bake for 20 minutes, until the cheese has melted. Serve cut in wedges with a green salad.

• Per serving 423 kcalories, protein 19g, carbohydrate 50g, fat 18g, saturated fat 7g, fibre 53g, added sugar none, salt 0.83g

Simple root vegetables combine with
blue cheese to make a satisfying supper.

Blue Cheese Vegetable Gratin

450g/1lb each of potatoes, carrots
and parsnips, thickly sliced
bunch of spring onions
large knob of butter
140g/5oz stilton
green beans, to serve

Takes 40 minutes • Serves 4

1 Preheat the oven to 200°C/Gas 6/fan oven 180°C. Cook the potatoes, carrots and parsnips in salted boiling water for 8–10 minutes, until just tender. Drain well.
2 Roughly chop the spring onions. Melt the butter in the pan you cooked the vegetables in (no need to wash it), add the spring onions and fry gently for a minute or two, until softened slightly. Tip in the vegetables and stir gently until coated with butter. Tip into a buttered shallow ovenproof dish.
3 Slice the cheese and arrange over the top of the vegetables. Bake for 20 minutes, until the cheese has melted. Serve hot straight from the oven, with green beans.

• Per serving 372 kcalories, protein 13g, carbohydrate 43g, fat 17g, saturated fat 10g, fibre 10g, added sugar none, salt 0.44g

This layered vegetable 'cake' makes a perfect alternative
to a roast joint. Serve with a veggie-friendly gravy.

Root Vegetable Bake

100g/4oz butter, softened
finely grated zest of 1 small lemon
2 garlic cloves, crushed
3 tbsp fresh thyme leaves
85g/3oz gruyère, finely grated
750g/1lb 10oz waxy
potatoes, peeled
225g/8oz celeriac, peeled
450g/1lb carrots, peeled
450g/1lb parsnips, peeled
and cored
vegetarian gravy, to serve

Takes 2 hours • Serves 6

1 Preheat the oven to 190ºC/Gas 5/fan
oven 170ºC. Use 25g/1oz butter to grease
a 20cm/8in cake tin (not loose bottomed).
Mash the remaining butter with the lemon
zest, garlic, thyme and gruyère. Season.
2 Very thinly slice the vegetables. Layer one
third of the potatoes, then celeriac, carrots
and parsnips in the tin. Dot with the butter.
Repeat the layers. Finish with black pepper
and dots of butter.
3 Cover the tin with foil and bake for
45 minutes. Remove the foil and bake for
a further 45 minutes until the vegetables are
tender. Leave for 5 minutes. Invert on to a
warm plate, place a plate over the top and
invert again so the crispy side is on top.
Serve with vegetarian gravy.

• Per serving 483 kcalories, protein 38g, carbohydrate
46g, fat 18g, saturated fat 5g, fibre 8g, added sugar
none, salt 8.3g

Choose a soft rindless goat's cheese
for this recipe.

Leek and Goat's Cheese Tarts

250g/9oz ready-made
shortcrust pastry
1 tbsp olive oil
1 leek, halved lengthways and cut
into 1cm/½in pieces
1 yellow pepper, seeded
and chopped
6 pitted black olives, quartered
2 tbsp fresh thyme leaves
100g/4oz soft rindless goat's
cheese, cubed
green salad or steamed winter
greens, to serve (optional)

Takes 45 minutes • Serves 4

1 Preheat the oven to 180°C/Gas 4/fan oven 160°C. Roll out the pastry on a lightly floured surface and use to line four 12cm/4½in loose-bottomed, fluted tart tins. Prick the pastry bases, line with greaseproof paper and fill with baking beans. Bake for 12 minutes.

2 Meanwhile, heat the oil in a large frying pan and fry the leek and pepper until softened. Remove the paper and baking beans from the tarts. Fill each tart with the leek and pepper mixture. Scatter over the olives, thyme and goat's cheese.

3 Cook for 10–12 minutes, until the pastry is golden and the cheese is slightly melted. Serve immediately with mixed salad leaves or freshly steamed winter greens, if liked.

• Per serving 441 kcalories, protein 9g, carbohydrate 38g, fat 29g, saturated fat 11g, fibre 3g, added sugar none, salt 1.68g

Frozen puff pastry makes a quick case
for a tangy, salty filling.

Red Onion, Feta and Olive Tart

25g/1oz butter
2 large red onions, finely sliced
2 tbsp light muscovado sugar
2 tbsp balsamic vinegar
flour, for dusting
450g puff pastry, thawed if frozen
100g/4oz feta, crumbled
175g/6oz black olives, pitted
and chopped
1 tbsp extra virgin olive oil
shredded basil leaves, to garnish
green salad, to serve

Takes 45 minutes • Serves 4

1 Preheat the oven to 200°C/Gas 6/fan oven 180°C. Heat the butter in a pan and add the onions. Add a pinch of salt and fry for about 10 minutes, until caramelised. Add the sugar and balsamic vinegar and cook for a further 5 minutes, until the juices are reduced and syrupy. Leave to cool.
2 Roll out the pastry on a floured surface and use to line a 30 × 22cm/12 × 8½in Swiss roll tin. Cover with the onion mixture and scatter over the feta and olives. Season and drizzle over the olive oil.
3 Bake for 15–20 minutes until the pastry is risen and golden and the base is crisp. Scatter over the basil leaves and cut into wedges. Serve with a green salad.

• Per serving 646 kcalories, protein 11g, carbohydrate 53g, fat 44g, saturated fat 18g, fibre 2g, added sugar 8g, salt 4.07g

Buy a ready-made pastry case to save time.
Try asparagus instead of the onions.

Cheesy Spring Onion Tart

1 bunch spring onions, trimmed
1 tbsp olive oil
225g/8oz soft goat's cheese
(eg, chevre), rind removed
150ml/¼ pint double cream
3 large eggs, separated
24cm/9½in ready-made shortcrust
pastry case
tomato salad, to serve

Takes 40 minutes • Serves 6

1 Preheat the oven to 190°C/Gas 5/fan oven 170°C and preheat the grill to hot. Place the spring onions on a baking sheet and brush with the oil. Grill for 2 minutes.
2 In a bowl, beat together the goat's cheese, cream and egg yolks until smooth. Whisk the egg whites until stiff and gently fold into the cheese mixture. Spoon into the pastry case and arrange the spring onions on top.
3 Bake for 20–25 minutes until golden. Serve with a tomato salad.

• Per serving 337 kcalories, protein 11g, carbohydrate 18g, fat 25g, saturated fat 13g, fibre 1g, added sugar 3g, salt 0.64g

Use your favourite curry paste,
rather than grind spices for this simple supper.

Creamy Egg Curry

2 tbsp oil
1 large, or 2 medium onions
(about 300g/10oz in total
weight), thinly sliced
2 heaped tbsp curry paste
230g can tomatoes
8 eggs
140g/5oz frozen peas
4 tbsp Greek-style yogurt
cooked rice and mango chutney,
to serve

Takes 45 minutes • Serves 4

1 Heat the oil in a frying pan. Add the
onion and cook for 10 minutes until golden.
Add the curry paste and cook, stirring, for
2 minutes. Add the tomatoes, 200ml/7fl oz
water and season. Bring to the boil, then
simmer for 20 minutes. Add a splash
of water if the curry becomes too thick.
2 Meanwhile, boil the eggs for 8 minutes.
3 Stir the peas and yogurt into the curry.
Simmer for 2–3 minutes. Peel and halve
each egg and gently stir into the curry.
Serve with cooked rice and mango chutney.

• Per serving 302 kcalories, protein 18g, carbohydrate
12g, fat 21g, saturated fat 5g, fibre 3g, added sugar
none, salt 0.84g

This rustic, peasant-style salad, traditional to southern Italy,
is packed with the flavour of sun-ripened vegetables.

Tuscan Salad

2 red peppers, seeded
and quartered
2 yellow peppers, seeded
and quartered
1 ciabatta loaf
6 tbsp extra virgin olive oil
3 tbsp red wine vinegar
2 garlic cloves, crushed
6 ripe plum tomatoes,
cut into chunks
50g/2oz caper berries or capers
50g/2oz marinated black olives
handful of fresh basil leaves,
roughly torn
2 tbsp pine nuts, toasted

Takes 35 minutes • Serves 4

1 Preheat the grill to hot. Grill the peppers
until charred and place in a plastic bag
so that the steam loosens the skins.
2 Meanwhile, tear the bread into rough
chunks, toast until golden brown and place
in a large bowl. Beat together the olive oil,
vinegar and garlic, season and set aside.
3 Remove the skin from the peppers and
cut into chunks. Toss with the toasted bread
along with the tomatoes, caper berries
or capers, olives, basil, pine nuts and the
dressing. Serve immediately on its own or
as an accompaniment to a creamy goat's
cheese or ripe brie.

• Per serving 622 kcalories, protein 15g, carbohydrate
69g, fat 33g, saturated fat 4g, fibre 5g, added sugar
none, salt 2.68g

Crisp, crunchy textures with fresh-tasting flavours
will make this speedy salad a firm favourite.

Orange and Celery Salad

2 large oranges
1 small head celery (about 350g/
12oz), trimmed, destringed
and sliced on the diagonal
1 small red onion, cut into
very thin wedges
225g/8oz red cherry
tomatoes, halved
85g/3oz lamb's lettuce
1 small garlic clove, crushed
2 tbsp chopped fresh mint
6 tbsp olive oil
1 tbsp balsamic vinegar

Takes 15 minutes • Serves 4

1 Cut away the peel and pith from the oranges. Cut each side of each membrane to remove the individual segments. Do this over a bowl to catch the juices.
2 Place the orange segments in a large serving bowl and sprinkle over the sliced celery, onion wedges, tomato halves and lamb's lettuce.
3 Add the crushed garlic, chopped fresh mint, olive oil and balsamic vinegar to the orange juice and whisk until well combined. Season to taste and pour over the salad. Toss well just before serving.

• Per serving 249 kcalories, protein 2g, carbohydrate 9g, fat 23g, saturated fat 3g, fibre 3g, added sugar none, salt 0.19g

A colourful winter salad
with a deliciously nutty dressing.

Warm Red Cabbage Salad

1 tbsp sunflower oil
1 red onion, sliced
1 small red cabbage (about 350g/
12oz), finely shredded
1 red apple, cored and cut
into chunks
1 carrot, grated
2 tbsp balsamic vinegar
½ tsp soft light brown sugar
½ tsp wholegrain mustard
4 tbsp walnut oil
2 little gem lettuces, roughly torn
50g/2oz walnut pieces
fresh flatleaf parsley, to garnish

Takes 25 minutes • Serves 4

1 Heat the oil in a frying pan and fry the onion for 1–2 minutes. Add the cabbage and cook for a further 2–3 minutes. Remove from the heat and add the apple and carrot.
2 Meanwhile, in a small bowl whisk together the vinegar, sugar, mustard and walnut oil. Season to taste.
3 Arrange the lettuce leaves on individual serving plates. Spoon the warm cabbage salad over. Sprinkle over the walnut pieces and drizzle over the dressing. Sprinkle over the flatleaf parsley and serve.

• Per serving 304 kcalories, protein 4g, carbohydrate 10g, fat 28g, saturated fat 3g, fibre 4g, added sugar 1g, salt 0.09g

Use buckwheat soba noodles for extra flavour and colour,
although egg noodles would be good, too.

Noodle and Watercress Salad

225g/8oz dried buckwheat
soba noodles
2 tbsp light soy sauce
2 tbsp sesame oil
4 tbsp saké (Japanese rich wine) or
dry white wine
2 tsp caster sugar
8 fresh mint leaves
1 large firm mango, halved,
stoned and peeled
85g/3oz watercress, stalks removed
2 tbsp sesame seeds, toasted
squeeze of lime juice

Takes 20 minutes • Serves 4

1 Cook the noodles in lightly salted boiling water according to the packet instructions, then drain and plunge immediately into cold water to refresh and stop the cooking process. Put the soy sauce, sesame oil, saké and sugar in a small pan and heat gently. Remove from the heat and stir in the mint. Set aside and allow to infuse.

2 Meanwhile, cut the mango into fine slivers. Drain the noodles thoroughly and toss with the soy sauce dressing, mango, watercress and half the sesame seeds.

3 Divide between four serving plates and sprinkle over the remaining sesame seeds. Squeeze over a little lime juice and serve immediately.

• Per serving 388 kcalories, protein 9g, carbohydrate 53g, fat 16g, saturated fat 2g, fibre 2g, added sugar 3g, salt 0.04g

A delicious combination of roasted fennel and zesty orange,
served on a bed of herby wheat.

Cracked Wheat and Fennel Salad

250g/9oz bulghar wheat
3 heads of fennel, cut into wedges
4 tbsp olive oil
pared zest and juice of 2 oranges
4 tbsp chopped fresh flatleaf parsley
2 tbsp chopped fresh mint
4 plum tomatoes, cut into wedges
140g/5oz mixed olives, drained
100g/4oz rocket

Takes 45 minutes • Serves 4

1 Preheat the oven to 200°C/Gas 6/fan oven 180°C. Place the bulghar wheat in a large bowl, cover with 1 litre/1¾ pints boiling water and allow to stand for 30 minutes. Meanwhile, place the fennel in a large roasting tin, drizzle with the olive oil and season. Add the orange zest and half the orange juice and roast in the oven for 35 minutes until softened and slightly charred.
2 Drain the bulghar wheat, add the parsley and mint and remaining orange juice. Combine well and season to taste. Place the tomatoes, olives and rocket in a large bowl, add the roasted fennel with the pan juices and toss well.
3 Divide the bulghar wheat between four serving plates, top with the fennel and tomato mixture and serve.

• Per serving 422 kcalories, protein 9g, carbohydrate 53g, fat 39g, saturated fat 5g, fibre 8g, added sugar none, salt 0.03g

So simple to make – serve this fresh-tasting pâté with crusty bread for a snack or light lunch.

Minty Broad Bean Pâté

500g/1lb 2oz broad beans, shelled weight, outer skins removed
1 garlic clove, very finely chopped
150ml/¼ pint extra virgin olive oil, plus extra for drizzling
pinch of ground cumin
small bunch fresh mint, chopped
8 slices crusty wholegrain bread, to serve

Takes 20 minutes, plus resting • Serves 4

1 Cook the broad beans in lightly salted boiling water for 10–12 minutes, until tender. Drain well, reserving the cooking water. Transfer the broad beans to a food processor, add the garlic and whizz to a purée, adding a few tablespoonfuls of the cooking water to give a soft consistency.

2 Preheat the grill to hot. Transfer the purée to a bowl and stir in the oil, cumin and mint. Season generously. Set aside for 30 minutes, if possible, to allow the flavours time to develop.

3 Toast each slice of bread on both sides and cut in half. Arrange on individual serving plates. Spoon the pâté on to the hot toast and drizzle over a little extra virgin olive oil.

• Per serving 413 kcalories, protein 7g, carbohydrate 9g, fat 39g, saturated fat 5g, fibre 8g, added sugar none, salt 0.03g

If you haven't got a griddle pan, simply stir fry the vegetables
and toast the bagel under a hot grill.

Bagels with Griddled Vegetables

5 tbsp olive oil
2 red peppers, seeded and
cut into chunks
2 courgettes, cut into thin slices
on the diagonal
4 onion bagels, split
2 tbsp balsamic vinegar
½ tsp sugar
70g bag wild rocket leaves

Takes 15 minutes • Serves 4

1 Brush a preheated griddle pan with a little of the oil. Add the peppers and courgettes and cook for 4–5 minutes, turning, until pleasantly charred. Transfer to a plate.
2 Toast the bagels, cut-side down, on the hot griddle pan for 1 minute, until golden. Meanwhile, to make a dressing, whisk the vinegar, sugar and remaining oil together. Season to taste.
3 Place the bagels on individual serving plates and top with the chargrilled vegetables and a handful of rocket. Drizzle the dressing over and serve immediately.

• Per serving 330 kcalories, protein 7g, carbohydrate 32g, fat 20g, saturated fat 3g, fibre 3g, added sugar 1g, salt 0.72g

Focaccia is a flat, round Italian bread, often sold flavoured with herbs, olives or sun-dried tomatoes.

Stuffed Focaccia

400g can chickpeas, drained and rinsed
juice of 1 lemon
1 garlic clove
5 tbsp extra virgin olive oil
20cm/8in round sun-dried tomato focaccia
100g/4oz semi-dried tomatoes in oil, drained
50g/2oz marinated black olives, pitted
30g bag of mixed salad leaves
1 small ripe avocado, halved, stoned, peeled and cut into chunks

Takes 15 minutes, plus chilling • Serves 6

1 For the houmous, whizz the chickpeas, half the lemon juice and garlic in a food processor until smooth. With the processor still running, drizzle in the oil steadily until combined. Season to taste.

2 Cut the focaccia into three horizontal layers of the same thickness. Spread the houmous over the bottom two layers and then scatter over the semi-dried tomatoes, olives and salad leaves.

3 Toss the avocado with the remaining lemon juice and season. Scatter over the topping, then reassemble the loaf. Chill for at least 15 minutes before cutting into wedges to serve.

• Per serving 305 kcalories, protein 8g, carbohydrate 27g, fat 19g, saturated fat 2g, fibre 4g, added sugar none, salt 1.27g

The walnut mixture will keep in an airtight container
for up to two days – just reheat it in a dry frying pan.

Walnut and Broccoli Spaghetti

350g/12oz spaghetti
225g/8oz broccoli,
broken into florets
4 tbsp olive oil
1 small onion, chopped
1 garlic clove, crushed
50g/2oz walnut pieces, chopped
50g/2oz fresh white breadcrumbs
½–1 tsp dried chilli flakes
1 tbsp walnut oil

Takes 20 minutes • Serves 4

1 Cook the spaghetti in lightly salted boiling
water for 5 minutes. Add the broccoli to the
pan, return to the boil and cook for a further
5 minutes until both are tender.
2 Meanwhile, heat half the oil in a frying
pan, add the onion and garlic and cook for
2 minutes until softened. Add the walnuts,
breadcrumbs, dried chilli flakes and walnut
oil and cook, stirring, until the crumbs are
crisp and golden brown.
3 Drain the pasta and broccoli in a colander.
Return to the pan, add the remaining olive
oil and stir to combine. Divide between
individual serving plates. Scatter over the
breadcrumb mixture and serve immediately.

• Per serving 633 kcalories, protein 17g, carbohydrate
79g, fat 30g, saturated fat 3g, fibre 5g, added sugar
none, salt 0.31g

You can use any pasta shape, but if you don't have any fresh available replace it with 350g/12oz dried pasta.

Pasta with Spicy Peas

3 tbsp olive oil
300g/10oz shallots, halved
4 tsp cumin seeds, lightly crushed
3 garlic cloves, sliced
300g/10oz cherry tomatoes, halved
good splash of Tabasco sauce
400g/14oz frozen petits pois
(or peas), thawed
finely pared zest and juice
of ½ lemon
500g/1lb 2oz fresh penne
4 tbsp chopped parsley

Takes 25 minutes • Serves 4

1 Heat the oil in a large pan. Add the shallots and cook for about 8 minutes, until softened and lightly coloured. Add the cumin and garlic and cook for a further 2 minutes.
2 Stir in the cherry tomatoes and cook for 5 minutes, until softened. Add the Tabasco sauce, petits pois or peas and lemon zest and juice. Season and cook for 2–3 minutes.
3 Meanwhile, cook the pasta according to the packet instructions and drain. Add the pasta to the peas and stir until well combined. Stir in the parsley and serve.

• Per serving 650 kcalories, protein 23g, carbohydrate 110g, fat 16g, saturated fat 2g, fibre 11g, added sugar none, salt 0.13g

Big on flavour but short on effort, this dish is suitable for vegans if you use egg-free pasta.

Pasta with Aubergines

5 tbsp olive oil, plus extra to serve
2 medium aubergines, diced
2 garlic cloves, finely chopped
2 tsp cumin seeds
1 red chilli, seeded and finely sliced
50g/2oz pine nuts, toasted
50g/2oz sultanas
350g/12oz tagliatelle (thin pasta ribbons)
6 tbsp chopped fresh coriander
zest and juice of 1 lemon
grilled lemon halves, to serve (optional)

Takes 25 minutes • Serves 4

1 Heat the oil in a large frying pan. Add the aubergines and cook gently, stirring occasionally, for 10 minutes until golden. Add the garlic, cumin and chilli, and cook for a further 4–5 minutes. Season to taste and add the pine nuts and sultanas.
2 Meanwhile, cook the pasta in lightly salted boiling water according to the packet instructions.
3 Drain the pasta thoroughly and add to the aubergine mixture, along with the coriander and lemon zest and juice. Toss together and serve with an extra drizzle of olive oil and grilled lemon halves, if liked.

• Per serving 627 kcalories, protein 15g, carbohydrate 79g, fat 30g, saturated fat 4g, fibre 6g, added sugar none, salt 0.07g

This simple Thai dish of noodles and vegetables in a tasty broth makes a satisfying supper.

Tom Yam Noodles

1 tbsp sunflower oil
1 small onion, chopped
2 garlic cloves
140g/5oz button mushrooms, sliced
1 red pepper, seeded and sliced
2 tsp vegetarian Thai red curry paste
700ml/1¼ pints vegetable stock
1 tbsp soy sauce
zest of 1 lime and juice of ½
125g/4½oz egg noodles
220g can bamboo shoots, drained
handful of fresh coriander

Takes 35 minutes • Serves 2

1 Heat the oil in a pan and fry the onion until golden. Stir in the garlic, mushrooms and red pepper and fry for 3 minutes. Add the Thai curry paste and cook for 1 minute. Stir in the stock, soy sauce and grated lime zest. Simmer for 3 minutes.
2 Add the noodles to the pan and bring to the boil. Simmer for 4 minutes, until they are cooked. Add the bamboo shoots and most of the coriander and cook for 2 minutes.
3 Divide the noodles between two soup bowls. Add the lime juice to the broth and season to taste. Pour over the noodles, scatter the remaining coriander over and serve.

• Per serving 393 kcalories, protein 15g, carbohydrate 55g, fat 14g, saturated fat 1g, fibre 7g, added sugar none, salt 2.77g

This salad is a riot of colours and contrasting textures and it's easily adapted to use whatever vegetables you have to hand.

Warm Crispy Noodle Salad

sunflower oil for deepfrying
50g/2oz crispy rice noodles
1 tbsp oil
2.5cm/1in piece fresh root ginger, chopped
2 garlic cloves, crushed
100g/4oz sugarsnap peas, sliced lengthways
1 carrot, cut into matchsticks
4 spring onions, sliced
175g/6oz spinach leaves, shredded
100g/4oz beansprouts
½ small cucumber, cut into matchsticks
50g/2oz roasted cashew nuts, chopped
juice of 1 lime
2 tsp chilli oil

Takes 30 minutes • Serves 2

1 Heat 5cm/2in of oil in a pan until a cube of bread browns in 30 seconds. Carefully add the noodles, a few at a time, and fry for a few seconds until puffed and crisp. Remove and drain on kitchen paper.
2 Heat one tablespoon of oil in a wok, add the ginger and garlic and stir fry for 30 seconds. Add the sugarsnap peas, carrot and spring onions and stir fry for 1 minute. Add the spinach and beansprouts and cook for a further minute, until wilted.
3 Remove from the heat, stir in the cucumber and season. Divide between serving plates and scatter the nuts and crispy noodles over. Squeeze over the lime juice, drizzle over the chilli oil and serve.

• Per serving 458 kcalories, protein 14g, carbohydrate 37g, fat 29g, saturated fat 2g, fibre 6g, added sugar none, salt 0.6g

A simple way to make everyday
vegetables taste out of the ordinary.

Spicy Coconut Vegetables

1 tbsp olive oil
1 onion, cut into wedges
1 red onion, cut into wedges
1 small red chilli, seeded
and chopped
2 carrots, sliced
225g/8oz small broccoli florets
1 red and 1 yellow pepper, seeded
and cut into chunks
200ml/7fl oz coconut cream
200ml/7fl oz vegetable stock
½ tsp Tabasco sauce
Thai fragrant rice, to serve

Takes 25 minutes • Serves 4

1 Heat the olive oil in a large pan and fry
the onion wedges and chilli for 1–2 minutes,
stirring occasionally.
2 Add the carrots, broccoli and peppers
and cook for a further 5 minutes.
3 Stir in the coconut cream, stock and
Tabasco sauce, reduce the heat and simmer
for 5 minutes. Serve immediately with Thai
fragrant rice.

• Per serving 400 kcalories, protein 7g, carbohydrate
14g, fat 36g, saturated fat 27g, fibre 11g, added
sugar none, salt 0.27g

This chilli uses ready-made sweet red pepper sauce, available from most supermarkets.

Bean and Vegetable Chilli

3 tbsp olive oil
2 onions, chopped
2 tsp caster sugar
250g/9oz chestnut mushrooms, sliced
2 garlic cloves, sliced
2 tsp mild chilli powder
1 tbsp ground coriander
290–350g jar sweet red pepper sauce
300ml/½ pint vegetable stock
410g can chickpeas, drained and rinsed
410g can black eye beans, drained and rinsed
boiled rice or crusty bread, to serve

Takes 55 minutes • Serves 4

1 Heat the oil in a large, heavy-based saucepan. Fry the onions and sugar over a high heat, until deep golden. Add the mushrooms, garlic, chilli powder and ground coriander and fry for 2–3 minutes.

2 Stir in the pepper sauce, stock, chickpeas and beans and bring to the boil.

3 Reduce the heat, cover and simmer gently for 20 minutes. Add a little extra stock if the mixture is too thick. Season and serve with boiled rice or crusty bread.

• Per serving 303 kcalories, protein 14g, carbohydrate 36g, fat 13g, saturated fat 2g, fibre 8g, added sugar 5g, salt 1.4g

This recipe is easily multiplied to feed a crowd.
The bean mixture can be made in advance and reheated.

Flageolet Bean Casserole

1 tbsp olive oil
3 medium courgettes,
cut into chunks
150ml/¼ pint dry white wine
2 × 300g cartons fresh tomato
pasta sauce
140g/5oz pitted black olives
2 × 400g cans flageolet beans,
drained and rinsed
2 tbsp chopped fresh rosemary
50g/2oz vegan spread
2 garlic cloves, crushed
2 tbsp chopped fresh flatleaf parsley
1 medium baguette, thickly sliced

Takes 40 minutes • Serves 4

1 Heat the oil in a large frying pan, add the courgettes and fry over a medium-high heat for 10 minutes, until softened and lightly charred.
2 Add the wine and boil rapidly for 2 minutes, until reduced by half. Add the tomato sauce, olives, beans and rosemary. Bring to the boil and simmer for 5 minutes. Season to taste.
3 Preheat the grill to high. Combine the vegan spread, garlic and parsley. Spread thickly on to the bread. Arrange the slices on the casserole and grill for 5–10 minutes, until golden.

• Per serving 546 kcalories, protein 24g, carbohydrate 61g, fat 22g, saturated fat 8g, fibre 15g, added sugar none, salt 4.35g

Vary the wine and lemon cream syllabub by the addition of different fruits in season.

Passion Fruit Syllabub

3 tbsp white wine
1 tbsp caster sugar
finely grated zest and juice of
1 small lemon
142ml carton double cream
1 passion fruit, cut in half
starfruit slices, to decorate
dessert biscuits, to serve (optional)

Takes 10 minutes, plus marinating •
Serves 2

1 Mix together the white wine, sugar and lemon zest and juice and leave for at least 30 minutes to marinate.
2 Pour the cream into the white wine mixture and, using an electric whisk, whip to soft peaks.
3 Scoop out the passion fruit flesh and seeds and stir lightly through the cream mixture. Spoon into two glasses or tumblers and decorate with the starfruit slices. Serve with dessert biscuits, if liked.

• Per serving 394 kcalories, protein 2.5g, carbohydrate 12g, fat 36g, saturated fat 22.5g, fibre 1g, added sugar 8g, salt 0.9g

This light, frothy mousse is at its best made with a high-quality dark chocolate.

Cappuccino Mousse

125g/4½oz plain chocolate
1 tbsp instant coffee granules
2 tbsp Tia Maria (coffee liqueur)
4 medium egg whites
140g/5oz caster sugar
300ml/½ pint double cream
cocoa powder, to dust

Takes 15 minutes, plus chilling • Serves 6

1 Melt the chocolate in a bowl set over a pan of simmering water, making sure the bowl doesn't touch the water. Remove from the heat and cool. Dissolve the coffee in two tablespoons of boiling water and stir in the Tia Maria. Stir into the chocolate.
2 In a bowl whisk the egg whites to soft peaks. Gradually whisk in the caster sugar until thick. Stir two tablespoonfuls of the meringue into the chocolate mixture to slacken it and then fold in the remainder. Spoon the mousse into six cappuccino cups and chill for at least 20 minutes.
3 Lightly whip the cream and spoon over the mousses. Dust with cocoa, to serve.

• Per serving 461 kcalories, protein 5g, carbohydrate 42g, fat 31g, saturated fat 19g, fibre 0.5g, added sugar 38g, salt 0.22g

Some supermarkets sell ready peeled and sliced
fresh pineapple, which will help to speed up this recipe.

Pineapple with Rum and Raisins

1 ripe pineapple, peeled
25g/1oz butter
50g/2oz light muscovado sugar
25g/1oz raisins
25g/1oz pecan nuts
50ml/2fl oz rum
vanilla ice cream, to serve (optional)

Takes 20 minutes • Serves 4

1 Remove the 'eyes' from the pineapple.
Cut in half, lengthways, remove the centre
core and slice into wedges. Melt the butter
in a griddle pan. Add the wedges of pineapple
and cook until golden – about 3 minutes on
each side.

2 Sprinkle over the sugar, raisins and pecan
nuts and cook until the sugar has melted
and becomes syrupy.

3 Carefully add the rum and ignite it, using
a long match. Allow the flames to die down.
Serve the pineapple wedges with the sauce
spooned over and a spoonful of vanilla ice
cream, if liked.

• Per serving 286 kcalories, protein 2g, carbohydrate
43g, fat 10g, saturated fat 3g, fibre 3g, added sugar
13g, salt 0.14g

Cut the richness of the mascarpone –
Italian cream cheese – by combining it with yogurt.

Mascarpone Cream with Grapes

150ml/¼ pint red wine
50g/2oz caster sugar
2 tsp arrowroot
350g/12oz seedless red, white or
black grapes
250g/9oz mascarpone cheese
225g/8oz Greek-style yogurt
2 tbsp clear honey

Takes 20 minutes, plus chilling •
Serves 4

1 Place the red wine and sugar in a large pan, bring to the boil and simmer, until the sugar has dissolved. Mix the arrowroot to a smooth paste with a little cold water, then stir into the wine. Boil, stirring continuously, for 1 minute, until thickened.

2 Stir the grapes into the wine mixture, bring to the boil, cover and simmer for 2 minutes. Leave to cool. Spoon into four tall glasses.

3 Put the mascarpone, yogurt and honey into a large bowl and whisk until smooth. Spoon over the grapes and chill until ready to serve.

• Per serving 487 kcalories, protein 0g, carbohydrate 35g, fat 34g, saturated fat 22g, fibre 1g, added sugar 19g, salt 0.58g

A creamy yogurt ice with far fewer calories than regular ice cream.
You'll find dried cranberries in larger supermarkets.

Cranberry Yogurt Ice

100g/4oz dried cranberries
finely grated zest and juice
of 1 orange
500ml/18fl oz Greek yogurt
50g/2oz caster sugar
150ml/¼ pint double cream
3 tbsp brandy

Takes 35 minutes • Serves 6

1 Put the cranberries, orange zest and juice and 150ml/¼ pint water in a pan, bring to the boil, cover and simmer for 25 minutes, until the cranberries are very soft. Allow to cool completely.

2 Beat together the yogurt, sugar and cream until the sugar has partially dissolved. Stir in the brandy and pour into a freezer-proof container. Freeze for 3 hours until thickened. Stir in the cranberry mixture until well distributed.

3 Freeze until solid. Transfer to the fridge for about 20 minutes before serving. Use within 2 months.

• Per serving 263 kcalories, protein 6g, carbohydrate 12g, fat 20g, saturated fat 12g, fibre 1g, added sugar 9g, salt 0.18g

A light raspberry and orange mixture is layered with
crunchy oat clusters to make a dairy-free dessert.

Raspberry Crunch Fool

300g/10oz raspberries,
plus extra for decorating
140g/5oz icing sugar
227g tub dairy-free cream cheese
400ml/14fl oz dairy-free yogurt
zest and juice of 1 orange
140g/5oz vegan oat clusters cereal
mint sprigs, to decorate

Takes 15 minutes, plus chilling •
Serves 4

1 Put one third of the raspberries in a food processor with half the icing sugar and whizz until smooth. Strain through a sieve to remove the pips.

2 Beat the dairy-free cream cheese, dairy-free yogurt, orange zest and juice in a bowl with the remaining icing sugar until smooth. Mix in the raspberry purée and fold in the remaining whole raspberries.

3 Divide half the mixture between four glasses. Sprinkle over half the cereal and spoon over another layer of the raspberry mixture. Sprinkle over the remaining cereal and decorate with sugar-dipped raspberries and sprigs of mint. Chill for 1 hour before serving.

• Per serving 565 kcalories, protein 20g, carbohydrate 76g, fat 22g, saturated fat 1g, fibre 2g, added sugar 44g, salt 1.46g

You'll find dairy-free yogurt and cream cheese
in large supermarkets or health food stores.

Peach Melba Brûlée

225g/8oz raspberries
140g/5oz icing sugar
300ml/½ pint dairy-free yogurt
227g tub dairy-free cream cheese
zest of 1 lemon
2 peaches, peeled, halved
and sliced
50g/2oz demerara sugar

Takes 25 minutes • Serves 4

1 Whizz half the raspberries in a food processor with 25g/1oz of the icing sugar until smooth. Place the remaining icing sugar, dairy-free yogurt, dairy-free cream cheese and lemon zest in a bowl and beat well together.

2 Preheat the grill to high. Divide the remaining raspberries and the peach slices between four 225ml/8fl oz ramekin dishes. Spoon over the raspberry purée.

3 Top with the yogurt mixture and sprinkle over the demerara sugar. Grill until the sugar has caramelised. Cool slightly before serving.

• Per serving 461 kcalories, protein 15g, carbohydrate 62g, fat 19g, saturated fat none, fibre 2g, added sugar 52.5g, salt 0.87g

A simple dessert with
the luxurious flavour of saffron.

Saffron Rice Pudding

large pinch of saffron strands
175g/6oz pudding rice
600ml/1 pint milk
300ml/½ pint double cream
125g/4½oz caster sugar
finely shredded zest and juice
of 2 lemons
lemon curd and biscuits,
to serve (optional)

Takes 35 minutes • Serves 4

1 Sprinkle the saffron over two tablespoons of hot water and leave to soak for 5 minutes.
2 Meanwhile, put the pudding rice, milk, cream, caster sugar and half the lemon zest into a large pan. Bring to the boil, then simmer gently for 20–25 minutes, until the rice is tender and the mixture has thickened. Stir in the saffron-infused water and lemon juice.
3 Spoon into serving bowls and sprinkle with the remaining shredded lemon zest. Serve with a spoonful of lemon curd and biscuits, if liked.

• Per serving 723 kcalories, protein 9g, carbohydrate 81g, fat 42g, saturated fat 26g, fibre 0.02g, added sugar 33g, salt 0.29g

Raid the fruit bowl and storecupboard
to make this satisfying pud.

Tropical Fruit Crunch

50g/2oz butter
100g/4oz rolled oats
6 tbsp demerara sugar
4 tbsp desiccated coconut
2 bananas, cut into chunks
2 ripe mangoes, peeled and
cut into chunks
225g can pineapple chunks in
natural juice, drained
fresh custard or single cream,
to serve

Takes 15 minutes • Serves 4

1 Melt two-thirds of the butter in a large frying pan. Sprinkle over the oats, four tablespoons of the demerara sugar and the desiccated coconut and cook for 3–4 minutes, stirring occasionally, until crisp and golden.

2 Meanwhile, melt the remaining butter in another frying pan and add the bananas, mangoes and pineapple chunks. Sprinkle over the remaining demerara sugar and cook over a low heat for 5 minutes, until softened and caramelised.

3 Divide the fruit between four plates and sprinkle over the crunchy oat mixture. Serve with fresh custard or single cream.

• Per serving 589 kcalories, protein 7g, carbohydrate 91g, fat 25g, saturated fat 16g, fibre 11g, added sugar 16g, salt 0.41g

This dessert looks spectacular, but made with just four ingredients, it has got to be one of the easiest to make.

Almond Nectarine Tart

140g/5oz white marzipan, cut into chunks
5 tbsp double cream
375g ready-made, ready-rolled puff pastry, thawed if frozen
4 nectarines, halved, stoned and thinly sliced
crème fraîche, to serve

Takes 30 minutes • Serves 8

1 Preheat the oven to 200°C/Gas 6/fan oven 180°C. Place the marzipan in a food processor with the cream and whizz to a thick paste. If necessary, roll the pastry out to a rectangle about 30 × 23cm/12 × 9in.
2 Lay the pastry on a baking sheet and score a line 2cm/¼in inside the edge all around. Spread the marzipan paste over the pastry inside the line and arrange the nectarine slices in rows on top.
3 Bake in the oven for 15–20 minutes, until the pastry is golden and risen. Cut into squares and serve with chilled crème fraîche.

• Per serving 311 kcalories, protein 4g, carbohydrate 34g, fat 18g, saturated fat 7g, fibre 1g, added sugar 9g, salt 0.39g

The addition of elderflower cordial to the gooseberry
filling gives the crumble an extra zing.

Gooseberry and Elderflower Crumble

550g/1lb 4oz gooseberries,
topped and tailed
175g/6oz caster sugar
3 tbsp elderflower cordial
75g/2½oz butter, diced,
at room temperature,
plus extra for greasing
175g/6oz plain flour
50g/2oz pecan nuts,
roughly chopped
fresh custard, ice cream or cream,
to serve

Takes 55 minutes • Serves 6

1 Preheat the oven to 190°C/Gas 5/fan oven 170°C. Grease a 1.2 litre/2 pint ovenproof dish. Put the gooseberries, two-thirds of the sugar and the elderflower cordial in a pan and cook gently for 5 minutes, until the fruit is soft. Transfer to the greased dish.
2 To make the crumble, rub the butter into the flour until the mixture resembles rough breadcrumbs. Stir in the remaining sugar and pecan nuts. Sprinkle over the goose-berries and level the surface. Bake for 30–40 minutes, until the topping is golden.
3 Divide the crumble between individual serving bowls and serve immediately with fresh custard, ice cream or pouring cream.

• Per serving 381 kcalories, protein 5g, carbohydrate 57g, fat 17g, saturated fat 7g, fibre 4g, added sugar 31g, salt 0.25g

A lovely autumn pudding that's easily adapted to use
most fruits in season. Serve with pouring cream.

Apple and Blackberry Pudding

75g/2½oz self-raising flour
75g/2½oz vegetable suet
100g/4oz white breadcrumbs
finely grated zest and juice of
1 large orange
5 tbsp milk
25g/1oz butter
1 large eating apple, peeled, cored
and roughly chopped
100g/4oz blackberries
100g/4oz caster sugar
pouring cream, to serve

Takes 55 minutes • Serves 6

1 Preheat the oven to 200°C/Gas 6/fan oven 180°C. Sift the flour into a bowl, stir in a pinch of salt, the suet, breadcrumbs, orange zest and just enough milk to make a soft crumble mix.
2 Melt the butter in a large frying pan and cook the apple for 5 minutes, until softened. Stir into the suet mix, then spread into a 1.2 litre/2 pint dish. Sprinkle the blackberries over.
3 Put the orange juice, sugar and 125ml/4fl oz water in a pan. Heat, stirring, until dissolved, then boil rapidly until pale golden. Pour over the pudding. Leave to soak for 10 minutes, then bake for 25 minutes. Serve hot or warm with pouring cream.

• Per serving 286 kcalories, protein 5g, carbohydrate 56g, fat 6g, saturated fat 3g, fibre 2g, added sugar 22g, salt 0.57g

Index

Picture credits and recipe credits

BBC Worldwide would like to thank the following for providing photographs. While every effort has been made to trace and acknowledge all photographers, we would like to apologise should there be any errors or omissions.

Chris Alack p21, p105, p159, p171, p179, p205; Marie-Louise Avery p65, p101; Iain Bagwell p87; Clive Bozzard-Hill p31, p59, p161, p203; Peter Cassidy p49, p125, p207, p211; Ken Field p13, p19, p47, p109, p117, p123, p129; Dave King p111, p139, p191; Richard Kolker p23, p37, p121; David Munns p25; Myles New p57; Thomas Odulate p39, p153, p195, p199, p201; William Reavell p11, p41, p107, p127, p133, p137, p151, p165, p181, p193, p197; Howard Shooter p15, p29, p163; Simon Smith p81, p97, p115, p155; Roger Stowell p27, p33, p35, p75, p77, p113, p145, p147; Sam Stowell p45, p157, p167, p209; Mark Thompson p131; Trevor Vaughan p53, 61, p71, p79, p99, p103, p135, p143, p149, p187, p189; Ian Wallace p43, p175; Simon Wheeler p67, p69, p85, p141, p185; Jonathan Whitaker p17, p55, p119; Frank Wieder p63, p73, p83, p89, p91, p93, p95, p177, p183; BBC Worldwide p51, p169, p173

All the recipes in this book have been created by the editorial teams on *BBC Good Food Magazine* and *BBC Vegetarian Good Food Magazine*.

Angela Boggiano, Lorna Brash, Sara Buenfeld, Mary Cadogan, Gilly Cubitt, Barney Desmazery, Joanna Farrow, Rebecca Ford, Silvana Franco, Catherine Hill, Jane Lawrie, Clare Lewis, Sara Lewis, Liz Martin, Kate Moseley, Orlando Murrin, Vicky Musselman, Angela Nilsen, Justine Pattison, Jenny White and Jeni Wright.